JOE
BIDEN

MEET THE
CANDIDATES
2020

JOE BIDEN

A VOTER'S GUIDE

Series Edited by
SCOTT DWORKIN

Compiled and Written by Grant Stern

Skyhorse Publishing

Introduction Copyright © 2019 by Scott Dworkin
Compiled and written by Grant Stern
All rights reserved. No part of this book may be reproduced in any manner
without the express written consent of the publisher, except in the case of brief
excerpts in critical reviews or articles. All inquiries should be addressed to
Skyhorse Publishing, 307 West 36th Street, 11th Floor, New York, NY 10018.
Skyhorse Publishing books may be purchased in bulk at special discounts for sales
promotion, corporate gifts, fund-raising, or educational purposes. Special editions
can also be created to specifications. For details, contact the Special Sales Department,
Skyhorse Publishing, 307 West 36th Street, 11th Floor, New York, NY 10018 or
info@skyhorsepublishing.com.
Skyhorse® and Skyhorse Publishing® are registered trademarks of Skyhorse
Publishing, Inc.®, a Delaware corporation.
Visit our website at www.skyhorsepublishing.com.
10 9 8 7 6 5 4 3 2 1
Library of Congress Cataloging-in-Publication Data is available on file.
Cover design by Brian Peterson

ISBN: 978-1-5107-5031-9
Ebook ISBN: 978-1-5107-5039-5
Printed in the United States of America

CONTENTS

JOE
BIDEN

INTRODUCTION TO JOE BIDEN

BY SERIES EDITOR SCOTT DWORKIN

n 2010, I was invited to Vice President Joe Biden's Christmas party at his official residence. Once I got through security, Dr. Jill and Joe Biden were there personally to greet me. We took some quick pictures together, and after I had a short conversation with the Bidens, I headed into the actual party.

Even though there were over a hundred people in the room, and even though it was packed, there were two things that really stood out to me. One was the fact that you could tell where Joe Biden was in the room at all times. He has a kind of energy that few politicians have; it resonates around you. And two, when you did bump into or talk to Biden, he was genuine, serious, but always seeming to have a positive outlook.

He was really happy guy that night, truly enjoying himself and the festivities for the holiday season. And he didn't just drop in and leave. He stayed around for a few hours. He hung out and was actually having a good time. He and I spoke again briefly about the holiday season, and then after a few hours, the party was over. It was a blast.

Joe Biden has a number of political strengths that will serve his 2020 primary campaign well. The personality and charisma he showed that night are chief among them.

The connection Biden makes with people is raw and genuine; it's his top strength. And it's so rare. It's no wonder he's running for president again. This is a time when the American people need someone who truly cares about America, a true patriot who has proudly served in elected office for nearly half a century.

The personal link Biden can form with voters on the campaign trail is one of the main things that sets him apart from the other candidates running. When Joe Biden speaks to individuals, it seems like those are the only people in the world who matter to him. I think that's truly the case. He has that kind of focus where he can set you apart from everything else and actually actively listen to what you've got to say. Plus, if you give him some kind of question or concern that he doesn't have an immediate answer to, the former vice president would make sure his staff actually follows up.

In addition to Joe Biden's ability to connect with people, he has a calming nature about him, a high energy level, and always seems to have a positive attitude—especially when he's faced multiple tragedies in his life, including the death of his first wife and his one-year-old daughter due to a car accident, only weeks after he won his first Senate campaign, and the tragic loss of his son Beau to brain cancer nearly forty-three years later while Biden was serving as vice president.[1] I can't think of many more tragic things that could happen to someone.

Still, Biden somehow managed to carry on with his duties as an elected official, and thrive. That shows true strength that's worthy of the presidency; it requires someone to adhere to a duty to serve these United States in the best way possible, in all ways, at all times, no matter what stands in your way.

Another strength of the former vice president's campaign is the fact he has become one of the most trusted names in American politics. That matters especially nowadays, with so many elected officials telling lies and committing corrupt acts. That, coupled with his name recognition and familiarity, will be a boon to his campaign. It's been one of the many things that's allowed his campaign to take off like a rocket ship early in the 2020 Democratic primary.

Unlike the 2008 and 2016 elections, where a fresh face and less political experience seemed to serve as a benefit for Obama and Trump, in 2020 Biden's depth of experience in politics will be a great benefit to his candidacy. Experience matters this election cycle. The American people want to know that they will have someone who can hit the ground running in the White House, someone who doesn't have a learning curve. There will be so much corruption to uncover, and so many things within the government to overhaul that Trump's damaged, that we will need a skilled political mind to help clean up the mess. Biden fits that bill.

While researching Biden's candidacy, I spoke to my good friend Lilly Ledbetter, the inspiration for the first bill President Obama signed into law, the Lilly Ledbetter Fair Pay Act. She told me that, "former Vice President Joe Biden is the most qualified person running for president. Biden has integrity, compassion, experience, and the love of our country. The president's job is not an-on-the-job training; they need to know how to do get to work the moment they're elected."

I also talked to another good friend of mine, Dr. Quincy Lucas, who, like Lilly, I had the pleasure of serving as an aide during President Obama's 2009 inaugural festivities. Dr. Lucas was responsible for nominating Joe Biden during the 2008 Democratic National Convention. He told me, "In a day and time where our country is in desperate need of a servant leader and a leadership team that is both humble and focused on human welfare for all—I place my trust in Joe Biden." He continued to say:

> Through my observations of and interactions with former Vice President Biden, I am confident in his ability to return our country to a place of stability. Joe Biden is intentional and unapologetic about his passion for service and commitment. As both an educator and advocate, I am interested in supporting individuals who are knowledgeable and courageous that will inspire change through best practices and action—Joe Biden will do just that!

As Lilly and Dr. Lucas noted, Biden's political experience is paramount for his campaign. It's going to be difficult for any other candidate to claim experience when standing next to him, although some of them are citing the need for change. It's the same age-old political rallying cry that Biden plied in his first 1988 presidential run and, twenty years later, propelled President Obama to the White House and Biden to living at the vice president's official residence at the U.S. Naval Observatory.

One of the biggest strengths in Biden's candidacy is something I call "The Obama Effect." His political partnership with former President

Obama was so unique that it will only benefit his standing in the race. He worked tirelessly for Obama, both on the campaign trail and in the White House. And people don't seem to forget that. Especially not Barack Obama.

Joe Biden is the only one who can say "I served as Obama's vice president" and "I served as Obama's right-hand man." That will matter, big time. People will want to recall the moments in time when America was on a successful path, when things like Obamacare was passed, which Biden was a big part of and famously called a "big f-ing deal." It was. They want to recall a time when the White House actually worked on behalf of the American people; where you had a vice president who believed that all American people are created equal. That's something that Americans are deeply longing for today with Donald Trump in the White House using presidential emergency powers to make random policy proclamations, often raising taxes on the poor and middle class with his beloved trade tariffs.

Biden's competitors in the primary will also have a hard time attacking his executive record, because if they attack him for that record then they're attacking former President Obama. We might see some people approach the line during debates or in attack ads, but we probably won't see anyone outright attack the vice president's record in office during the primary. It is possible someone could say, "Well, that was Obama, that wasn't you." That definitely wouldn't breed positive news headlines. And attacking President Obama in any way surely won't help anyone gain in the polls.

If someone actually decided to fiercely attack Joe Biden's record from 2009 to 2017, all it would do is bring President Obama out to defend him.

And whoever makes that attack, their campaign probably won't recover from the blowback. That's how powerful the Obama Effect will be for Joe Biden in this campaign.

It will be a centerpiece to everything, especially in Biden's television advertisements. Because why wouldn't you talk about the days that were before Trump, and how you can continue Obama's vision—and mention Obama's name as much as you possibly can? Plus, Joe Biden can tell his personal stories of all the times he had to make tough decisions with Obama. There are so many great examples of Biden's leadership while in the White House, like being in on the decision-making process for the raid that killed Osama bin Laden. It's safe territory for the loquacious former senator from Delaware to tell stories, including the story of how he managed to dramatically limit his former penchant for political gaffes over the course of an eight-year term in office.

The Obama Effect on Biden's campaign is priceless, and it's not something anyone can duplicate. No one else has those experiences. No one else can put us in touch with where we were before as a country, outside of Obama himself, more than Joe Biden. And he deserves a lot of credit for serving in the role. It was really the zenith of his political career to date, and unlike his other previous high-profile moments, it wasn't a mixed result. It was a win.

He grew from a lawmaker into a statesman and an excellent, bipartisan leader. Biden led the campaign to get the votes in Congress to pass Obamacare; he was a lead negotiator with Republicans on the hill during budget talks and led international trips to war zones. That's probably one of the reasons why President Obama gave Joe Biden high praise as "the best vice president America has ever had."[2]

Joe Biden has been always been a key diplomat for America. This is another example of an area where experience matters, in both domestic and international politics. He's got a track record that counts, and it's extensive—not just his time in the White House, but also his thirty-six years in the United States Senate.

Another powerful strength for the Biden campaign arises from his extensive connections within the entire Democratic Party. People don't forget when you help them out, especially folks in the Democratic Party. He's campaigned for many elected Democrats when they really needed the help; he's helped many Americans from all walks of life, all throughout the country. All of it is already starting to pay off for his campaign in dividends, with widespread financial support and in retaining a seasoned campaign staff from the outset of the contest. It's no surprise he already has fifteen endorsements from members of Congress.

Rep. Al Lawson (D-FL) endorsed Biden's campaign in early June 2019. "They don't make 'em like Joe anymore," said the African American representative from northeast Florida's Jacksonville. He continued.[3]

> We have an opportunity now to meet head on the greatest challenges of our time, and ensure our best days still lie ahead of us and that is why I am endorsing him to be the next president of the United States. He has a long history of doing what's right and not what's easy to

> *advance the causes of America's working families. And a*
> *proven track record of bringing people together and deliv-*
> *ering results. America is at a crossroads and it is vital*
> *that we elect a leader who will restore the soul of this*
> *country, put us back on a path of prosperity and make*
> *certain we are respected on the world stage. I have no*
> *doubt that Vice President Biden is that leader.*

That's one stellar endorsement. But I think it encapsulates a lot of the reasons folks have been so fond of the former vice president's candidacy this time around in a way that he never achieved in his first two campaigns to make it into the Oval Office.

The last strength for Joe Biden I want to outline is crucial. As of now, Democratic leadership in the House and Senate believe that a Biden candidacy is the best chance Democrats have at keeping the House and taking back the Senate and the White House. He could turn that into a big selling point for Democratic primary voters. And Biden's battle-tested. He's been on this road before.

Although Biden clearly has the strongest campaign at the moment, there are some things that can cause him trouble down the road.

In the past, plenty of presidential candidates who were considered front-runners eventually had failing campaigns. It's going to be a tough battle for Biden to stay on top, but it might make things easier having so many other candidates in the race. People might not evaluate twenty-three different presidential candidates. They might not research everyone, or go through the trouble of reading each book in our series. They might just go with their gut. And right now it looks like the gut winner would be Biden. But again, presidential front-runners have failed in the past.

As long as Biden doesn't commit major gaffes and avoids any sort of campaign controversy, he should be fine. But he already is being attacked by Trump and other Republicans for a number of things. One example is everything related to his handling of the Anita Hill hearings. Hill came forward to testify against Clarence Thomas during his Supreme Court confirmation process and accused Thomas of sexually harassing her in the workplace.[4] Since Biden was chair of the Senate Committee on the Judiciary at the time; he had the ability to present corroborating witnesses, didn't intervene when she was attacked by other Senators, and was critical of her in his own questioning. It has reflected poorly on Biden, though he has apologized to Hill, and will undoubtedly continue to haunt him during debates.

The most recent attacks on Biden have been regarding his leadership in pushing through the 1994 crime bill, which funded prisons, made sentences more severe, and led to mass incarceration throughout the country.[5] However, the bill did ban various assault weapons, led to new laws for sex offender registries, and also included the Violence Against Women Act. So he will be able to debate its positives in the bill as well.

Something else that will definitely come up is Biden's record on civil rights, especially his former antibusing stance. He fought the busing of African American students into predominantly white neighborhoods as a method for desegregation of schools for years while in the Senate.[6] Even though this was nearly fifty years ago, it could prove to be a deal breaker for some voters.

But at least Biden is trying to right his wrongs. When Trump attacked Biden for making some women and men uncomfortable, Biden responded by saying: "The boundaries of protecting personal space have been reset. I get it. I get it. I hear what they're saying and I understand it. I'll be much more mindful. That's my responsibility and I'll meet it."[7]

Overall, like most people, Biden has some dirty laundry. But it seems to have been all aired out over the years. And it doesn't even come close to the controversies and corruption surrounding Trump. But the negatives do exist, and they do pose a problem if some of these issues resurfaced.

Can Joe Biden win the 2020 Democratic primary? I think it's very clear that Biden can absolutely, without a doubt, win.

In order for him to win the primary, he will have to do a number of things well, including something very simple but challenging: he has to be able to appeal to the further left in the Democratic Party. The progressives, people like me in the Resistance. And he has some deep progressive credentials he can tout. Whether it's his push for universal health care, his leadership for years on the issue of climate change, or his support for organized labor, Biden must emphasize this experience on the campaign trail and use it to answer charges that he is too moderate during debates. Still, one of the only ways to get true liberals on board for good might be to add one to his ticket if he's the nominee. It will be otherwise tough to pull them away from stalwart progressives like Senators Warren, Harris, and Sanders, and unite the left behind him should he become the nominee.

Biden will also have to not commit any unforced errors. And he really needs to demonstrate that he learned from past mistakes. If he doesn't, it will reopen old wounds that took a long time to heal.

The debates will be pivotal for his campaign. They can help him build unstoppable momentum for the primary season. Although his last presidential campaign ended early, pundits agreed that he demonstrated real prowess during the numerous debates of the 2008 primary.

In order to win the Democratic presidential nomination, Biden will also have to hold on to his massive early lead, something that most candidates have failed to do. Hillary Clinton in 2008 is a prime example, eventually losing to Barack Obama. Right now Biden is polling above Senator Bernie Sanders, Senator Elizabeth Warren, and Senator Kamala Harris combined.

It's clear that Joe Biden can win the primary, but can he beat Trump? I think that Biden can mop the floor with Trump in the general election. I personally believe that it would be a landslide victory for Biden. You can tell from Trump's attacks on Biden that Trump views Biden as his biggest threat. Biden is one of the few candidates that Trump thinks can beat him.

Joe Biden would make a great president. Biden is not someone who is going to tweet a bunch of nonsense, or threaten journalists at his rallies. He is always going to be more rational than Trump, even on his worst day. He would be fair, honest, and he'd actually do what's best for the American people—not what's best for him, his wallet, or his personal business ties. America would be lucky to have Joe Biden back in the White House, this time as president of the United States.

WHO IS JOE BIDEN?

Vice President Joe Biden has led in the 2020 Democratic primary polls from the start of the race, even while he waited to formally declare his candidacy until the relatively late date of April 25, 2019. He's is often characterized as the prototypical, personable Irish politician, and looking to make his third time running the charm in the 2020 race for America's top job.

Joe Biden's lengthy public service career started early with his election to the Senate just before turning thirty years old. But it took him seven terms in the Senate lasting thirty-six years before he earned near-universal acclaim. Eight months after ending his second bid for the presidency, he accepted Barack Obama's nomination as the Democratic nominee for vice president.

Biden redefined the office of the vice president during his years living at Number One Observatory Circle. President Obama assigned him an extremely active role atop numerous key administration initiatives, from overseeing stimulus funds for infrastructure to being its top decision maker about the war in Iraq.

Early in the 2020 Democratic primary race, Biden's effusive popularity in the Democratic party is due to his eight years with President Barack Obama and the comforting return to normalcy he represents. Joe Biden is a true American statesman, and a longtime DC insider, but one whose "Amtrak Joe" nickname best personifies how he never lost touch with life outside the Washington Beltway. Those eight years have become Joe Biden's defining moments in modern politics.

Before his national political career could begin in earnest after winning a surprise election against a longtime Republican politician at the age of twenty-nine, the Delaware senator-elect suffered a life-altering tragedy. Joe Biden would be sworn into office at a hospital where he attended to his two sons, Beau and Hunter, having lost his first wife and daughter to an collision between her car and a tractor trailer during a routine shopping trip.

Senator Biden buried himself in work and rebounded personally when he met a beautiful schoolteacher named Jill Jacobs, remarrying just under five years after the accident. His early years would be marked by a pragmatic break from his early aspirational policies, which were guided by his constituents' loud demands. In 1975, he joined the Senate Committee on Foreign Affairs, and soon afterward the newly formed Senate Intelligence Committee.

Later, Biden joined the powerful Senate Committee on the Judiciary which oversees all federal nominations to the bench. From that post, where he became the ranking member in 1981 and chairman in 1987 through 1994, the senator would participate in, sponsor, and draft his most consequential legislation; much of it revolved around crime, including a pair of sweeping crime bills in 1984 and 1994. However, those bills came with mixed results.

Senator Biden declared his candidacy for president the first time in 1987, while holding the chair of the judiciary committee. His campaign unraveled three months before the first votes in a plagiarism scandal that happened right when the national media spotlight was on him for his senatorial duties in one of the highest-profile Supreme Court nominations to ever fail. Biden quit the presidential race with dignity, and "won" the nomination hearings by defeating President Reagan's nominee, who was widely believed to be a capricious jurist. The incident stifled his long-standing presidential ambitions for two decades, but his colleagues in the Senate rallied around him in bipartisan fashion, and the improbable end result strengthened his position as Delaware's senator.

Only months after he retired from the presidential race, Senator Biden faced a serious health crisis when a blood vessel in his brain ruptured due to an aneurysm. Against fifty-fifty odds of survival, Joe Biden returned to his duties only six months later, in decent health that continues through today. He has long said that had he continued to run for president, he might not have sought treatment and could've died.

Biden's senatorial career for the next twenty years included numerous high-profile judicial fights that have shaped American politics and particularly the way we view sexual harassment in the workplace. His legislative powers reached their peak with the 1994 crime bill, a bill with landmark programs and some equally consequential failures. By the mid-1990s, the senator's focus turned to foreign affairs, and he became the Senate Foreign Affairs Committee's ranking member in 1997, then later its chairman for two terms of two years each in 2001–2003 and 2007–2009. Biden's votes on the Iraq war (against the 1991 resolution to use force, for the 2002 resolution to use force) have been endlessly analyzed. By the end of his last chairmanship, Biden proposed an Iraq plan that aged rather well, but his 2008 presidential candidacy is what led him to an immersive focus on the Middle East.

He didn't win the Democratic presidential nomination, but Barack Obama picked Biden as his running mate. After a tumultuous but victorious campaign by a wide margin, President Obama gave Vice President Biden the Iraq portfolio to manage, while he concentrated on the numerous problems at home stemming from the crash of the economy during the George W. Bush administration, resulting financial crisis, and the "Great Recession." The vice president was also assigned to oversee Obama's largest program of his first term: the Recovery Act, which stimulated the economy with hundreds of billions of dollars in spending.

Joe Biden had a successful eight years as vice president by any metric, becoming President Obama's right-hand man and key adviser. However, he suffered a great tragedy during those years when his eldest son, Beau Biden, passed away suddenly from an aggressive form of brain cancer. The vice president grieved in private, and ultimately, it was one of the main reasons he chose not to run for president in 2016.

Now, Joe Biden is back in the political fray for his third attempt to capture the Democratic nomination. If elected, he would be the oldest first-term president in American history, a feat only one other challenger, Senator Bernie Sanders, is attempting in the twenty-three person Democratic primary field. Because of his age, Biden boasts the most impressive résumé in the field, but also the challenge of running as an aging white male at a time when many Democratic voters clamor for a change in representation.

As the early front-runner in the race, Joe Biden faces the difficult task of leading the primary field from start to finish, with so many other challengers. It's a Herculean task, but perhaps one that the former senator and vice president is up to conquering. If he does, he'll face off against Donald Trump in the 2020 election—a matchup he, more so than his fellow Democratic contenders, is favored to win.

DEFINING MOMENTS IN JOE BIDEN'S POLITICAL CAREER

The moments that most define Joe Biden's political career happened in August 2008, when Barack Obama tapped the senator from Delaware and former primary rival to become his vice presidential running mate. In the last fifteen years, it is still Biden's most Google-searched moment, even more so than his 2019 presidential primary launch.[1]

Ironically, Biden grew to become friends with Senator Obama after a flubbed comment he made about the junior senator from Illinois hindered his own presidential primary campaign right out of the gate. Obama also served on the Senate Foreign Relations Committee—where they hadn't been close—while on the grueling campaign trail, which featured seventeen debates between the candidates before the Iowa caucuses.[2]

THE 2016 PRESIDENTIAL ELECTION

Barack Obama chose Senator Biden for his foreign policy experience, his touch with working-class voters, and penchant for going on the attack. On

August 23, 2008, Obama announced Biden's nomination during the run-up to the Democratic National Convention in Denver.[3]

At the convention, Joe Biden addressed the assembled party members on August 27, 2008, saying, "Since I've never been called a man of few words, let me say this as simply as I can: Yes. Yes, I accept your nomination to run and serve alongside our next president of the United States of America, Barack Obama," according to NPR.[4] He continued:

> You can learn an awful lot about a man campaigning with him, debating him, and seeing how he reacts under pressure. You learn about the strength of his mind, but even more importantly, you learn about the quality of his heart.
>
> I watched how [Barack Obama] touched people, how he inspired them, and I realized he has tapped into the oldest American belief of all: We don't have to accept a situation we cannot bear. We have the power to change it. That's Barack Obama, and that's what he will do for this country. He'll change it.

"These are extraordinary times," concluded Biden. "This is an extraordinary election. The American people are ready. I'm ready. Barack Obama is ready. This is his time. This is our time. This is America's time."

The vice president's traditional role on the campaign trail is the "attack dog," which allows the presidential nominee to remain above the fray, making a positive case for the nomination. Biden's speech slammed Senator John McCain (R-AZ) for voting against raising the minimum wage nineteen times, and saying that the war in Afghanistan was going well when it really wasn't.[5, 6]

When Joe Biden was chosen to be Obama's running mate, the American economy was in crisis. The stock market's Dow Jones Industrial Average—representing America's blue-chip stocks—was in the 8,800 range, down a stupendous 37 percent from its high just short of 14,000 just one year earlier, due to the subprime mortgage meltdown caused by Wall Street's tragic underwriting standards for securities.[7] The national unemployment rate was up to 6.1 percent of adults seeking work who could not find a job, increased 25 percent from the 4.6 percent rate just a year earlier.[8] One of the largest Wall Street investment banks, Bear Stearns, had already failed, and another even larger institution, Lehman Brothers, was teetering on the brink of collapse. During George W. Bush's years in the White House, the U.S. economy was fueled by massive tax cuts to the rich, which Biden staunchly opposed, and a toxic cocktail of bank deregulation and debt.

The Obama/Biden ticket had to navigate a series of unprecedented situations, including a last-minute White House meeting with congressional leadership to discuss the Bush administration's bailout of Wall Street on the literal eve of the first presidential debate.[9] Six days later, both senators, Biden and Obama, had to return to DC to cast votes in favor of the Bush administration's $700 billion Troubled Asset Relief Program. Two days after that, President Bush signed the bank bailout into law on the day of the one and only vice presidential debate. As expected, Joe Biden ran circles around his inexperienced Republican foe, Gov. Sarah Palin (R-AK), whose most memorable line was asking the senator if she could call him "Joe." She openly refused to answer questions posed by Gwen Ifill of PBS, preferring to give a political speech during a debate. CNN viewers said that Biden won the debate by a fifteen-point margin.[10]

Joe Biden demonstrated good political discipline during the 2008 general election campaign. He had the awkward interview here and there, and rather embarrassingly, but not consequentially, instructed a Missouri state senator to "get up" during the rousing conclusion of one of his speeches—but Sen. Chuck Graham is disabled, so Biden told his audience to stand up for the senator.[11] The only major question about his candidacy was his health, due to a pair of brain aneurysms he survived in the late 1980s. But doctors gave Senator Biden a clean bill of health.[12]

VICTORY

On Election Day, November 4, 2008, Barack Obama and Joe Biden defeated John McCain and Sarah Palin by over 9.5 million votes, a resounding 7.2 percent margin of victory in the popular vote.[13] The Obama/Biden campaign had raised a startling amount of money to get across the finish line: three quarters of a billion dollars, more than double what the GOP nominees took in. Most importantly, Obama and Biden won 365 votes in the treacherous electoral college to McCain and Palin's 173 votes—a blowout. (Eight years later, Hillary Clinton won 2.9 million more votes, but lost in the electoral college by seventy-seven votes, the second time in five elections that the archaic electoral college contradicted voter will, resulting in a president elected with a minority of the votes.[14])

Later, Bureau of Labor Statistics data showed that just during the course of the 2008 presidential campaign, the U.S. unemployment rate rose from

6.1 percent to 6.8 percent, an increase of greater than 10 percent in just a few months. In 2007, the economy grew by 1.9 percent but in 2008, growth turned negative to 0.1 percent. The two Democrats inherited an economy that contracted by a whopping 2.8 percent in 2009.

The president-elect maintained an unusually high profile during the transition period, effectively taking the bully pulpit from lame duck President Bush during the holiday season. Both Obama and Biden used their seats in the Senate, which introduced legislation on January 6, 2009, to build a major stimulus package in Congress, intended to jumpstart the economy soon after inauguration.

INAUGURATION

On a bitterly cold day, over 1.1 million Americans trekked to Washington, DC, to see Barack Obama and Joe Biden sworn in. The cautiously optimistic crowd filled the National Mall as far as the eye could see. At the time, nobody realized that the Great Recession was going to get a lot worse before it would get better. Supreme Court Justice John Paul Stevens swore in Vice President Biden as the first Roman Catholic and first Delawarean to hold that office.

BIDEN BECOMES THE VICE PRESIDENT

Vice President Joe Biden became President Obama's right-hand man while in office, with the two men enjoying an unusually close relationship. Obama gave Biden high praise early on by comparing him to a "glue guy" in basketball: someone whose effort makes the team win, but unselfishly isn't about getting the credit. President Obama described the vice president as a team player "who does a bunch of things that don't show up in the stat sheet," the president said in a March 2009 interview to the *New York Times*. "He gets that extra rebound, takes the charge, makes that extra pass."[15]

The result became the American Recovery and Reinvestment Act of 2009.[16] President Obama signed the Recovery Act, also known as the "Obama stimulus," into law just twenty-seven days into his term of office. It was a bill designed to funnel as much cash into "shovel ready" projects that were awaiting funding in local and state governments across the country. Vice President Biden was placed in charge of oversight for the massive $787 billion spending plan, along with an advisory board and a group of eleven inspectors general.[17] After three years, the fraud rate was under 1 percent and Biden handed off his oversight duties, telling ABC News, "Through the Recovery Act, we've proved that the government can move quickly and get the job done and do it right."[18] Forty-four days after Obama and Biden took office, the stock market hit bottom at 55.4 percent of its original value. Soon afterward, the administration launched an ambitious mortgage refinancing plan called the Home Affordable Refinance Program that let millions of homeowners take advantage of plunging interest rates to save money by refinancing into what many called the "Obama loan."[19]

In late April 2019, Vice President Biden pulled off a political coup de main against the Republican Party's senate minority when he convinced Arlen Specter, a moderate longtime senator from Pennsylvania, to switch parties, giving Democrats a filibuster-proof sixtieth vote in the upper chamber.[20] Biden worked on Specter, whose state neighbors Delaware, for a hundred days. It represented a seismic power shift in the federal government with unified Democratic control of all three political branches of government. Regrettably, events like freshman Senator Al Franken's (D-MN) long fight to win his 2008 election and health issues like the liberal lion Senator Ted Kennedy's (D-MA) brain cancer and subsequent death would rob Obama and Biden of the fruits of their hard-won political fights just as Republicans regrouped with a major new propaganda campaign called the "Tea Party."

In October 2009, unemployment peaked at 10.2 percent and the Democratic congressional majority in both houses was struggling to hold hearings on and draft health-care legislation, which would later turn out to be President Obama's crowning achievement. In the short run, it was a political catastrophe; the GOP and conservative media outlets like Fox News railed against "death panels" and worked to turn public opinion against the initiative. But Democrats were diligently working out the details of eliminating preexisting health issue screening, determining a list of essential health benefits, and crafting the mechanism to make state and federal insurance exchanges to promote market competition among plans. The *New Republic* reported that at one low point, the vice president argued that it was time to end the effort, but President Obama stayed the course and in March 2010, the Patient Protection and Affordable Care Act became law.[21, 22]

At the bill signing ceremony, an open mic caught Vice President Biden uttering his most immortal political gaffe, which came on live television as the assembled crowd in the White House burst into applause when he introduced the president after he signed the ACA. "This is a really big fucking deal," Biden told Obama, embracing his boss.[23] He was right, it still is. The ACA has only grown in popularity since its rocky implementation in 2014 and Republican threats to kill coverage of preexisting conditions. Biden is certain to bring up health care throughout the election as it's one of his strongest political legacies.

From early in his first term, the vice president quickly became the Obama administration's point man on Iraq, visiting the country every two months. "Joe, you do Iraq," the president famously told Biden.[24]

President George W. Bush had signed a status of forces agreement (SOFA) before Obama took office, and it committed America to withdrawing most of its troops by 2011. Vice President Biden had opposed the "troop surge" plan in Iraq, but had to implement it before he later oversaw the U.S. Army's withdrawal. It was a difficult portfolio to manage, considering that the outgoing lame duck president had committed the new administration's hand, but he carried out the task with aplomb, predicting that extricating America from Iraq could prove to be one of the administration's great successes.[25] Particularly, Joe Biden's diplomacy was necessary in 2010 when the Iraqi government extralegally disqualified hundreds of political candidates and he successfully restored fifty-nine of their campaigns.[26]

Unfortunately, events dating back to the early days of the George W. Bush administration caused the birth of a terrorist organization called ISIS or ISIL, which festered for years until becoming a territorial power called the "Islamic State," which American forces defeated in combat to end its territorial holdings in the waning days of the Obama administration and early in the Trump regime.[27] However, the group is still lurking in Iraq and Syria looking to make a comeback to this day.[28]

In 2013, Joe Biden had to deal with a major health scare in his immediate family when his eldest son, Beau, was stricken with brain cancer.[29] Beau Biden was an Iraq war veteran and former assistant U.S. attorney who had become Delaware's attorney general, and a rising political star in his own right. Three years earlier, Beau had suffered a minor stroke, and again, he managed to recover from the life-threatening illness at the world-renowned University of Texas MD Anderson Cancer Center, where a lesion was removed from his brain. By 2014, he had returned to public life, bouncing back quickly, but questions about his health remained.[30]

The end of Biden's term was consumed by countering Russia's hybrid-war against Ukraine. He was on personal terms with its pro-Kremlin President Viktor Yanukovych, who spent years dancing between Moscow and the EU. Ukraine's president hired a American political operative named Paul Manafort to run his political strategy, and he implemented a wedge-issue campaign between the Russian-leaning east and the European-leaning west of the country. Manafort later became President Trump's campaign chairman and pleaded guilty to criminally deceiving the Obama administration on important matters of state between the two nations after Special Counsel Robert Mueller indicted him on a laundry list of charges and secured an eight-count conviction in federal court.[31]

The vice president called Yanukovych frequently during the February 2014 protests that would lead to his ouster, seeking to promote a reconciliation between the head of state and his people, but to no avail.[32] The embattled Ukrainian president ordered government troops to fire on protesters, then fled to Russia as the protesters closed in on the Maidan aka Independence Square. The resulting Euromaidan Revolution changed Kiev's government without much more bloodshed, and Biden visited two months later, when the Maidan was still half destroyed and Ukraine was barely surviving as an independent nation, though one with a raging Russian-led insurgency happening on its eastern side.[33]

In the spring of 2015, Beau Biden's cancer returned with a vengeance, and he entered the Walter Reed Hospital in Bethesda, Maryland, which had saved his father's life twenty-seven years previously.[34] Tragically, Joe Biden's forty-six-year-old son passed away on May 30, 2015. "Beau Biden was, quite simply, the finest man any of us have ever known," his devastated father wrote in a statement to the press. "The entire Biden family is saddened beyond words."[35]

Vice President Biden mourned his loss in private, and with the end of his term of office rapidly approaching, he had to make a decision about whether to run for president in 2016 or to sit out the race. As he and President Obama became lame-duck executives after a devastating midterm election loss in 2014, they also had to contend with the deteriorating situation in Iraq and Syria, which led to a slew of high-profile terror attacks throughout Europe.

Ultimately, Joe Biden chose to leave public life in 2017, a difficult choice, but one that his family agreed upon. His grief was too great, and former Secretary of State Hillary Clinton's presidential ambitions too strong, to permit him to attempt a presidential run. President Obama wasn't behind the idea of a presidential run, either, and, after all, Biden had previously said he wouldn't seek a new term of office after the vice presidency.

Joe Biden left office on January 20, 2017, with an approval rating of 61 percent, according to Gallup.[36] His valedictory represented a peak in public appreciation of the longtime senator and vice president, but it would be Secretary Clinton's devastating electoral loss in 2016 that would set Biden on the path toward running for president a third time.

POLICY: CAMPAIGN PLATFORMS

Vice President Biden is running what most observers consider to be a "biographical" campaign, which isn't as heavy in policy as his opponents. Senator Biden's career shows him to be a pragmatic, rather than ideological, domestic policy maker, moving his vision alongside the desires of his constituencies.

His campaign website doesn't have any specifics, but lists an agenda of Joe's "Vision for America," with his top three issues and thirteen principles by which he promises to govern the nation:

1. We've got to rebuild the backbone of the country: the middle class.
2. We've got to demonstrate respected leadership on the world stage.
3. We've got to make sure our democracy includes everyone.[1]

Biden's largest issue is rebuilding the middle class—people who expect to get ahead while "playing by the rules" and achieving long-term success, people such as teachers, nurses, police officers, and firefighters, who perform some of the most critical tasks in America. His platform starts with "restoring the basic bargain for American workers" which talks about the vast disparity between the expanding salaries of CEOs and the stagnant wages of average workers.

Joe Biden's plan to guarantee "every American the skills and education they need to get ahead" is one of his most detailed policy proposals, and it is for K-12 education. If elected, he promises to:

- Support our educators by giving them the pay and dignity they deserve.
- Invest in resources for our schools so students grow into physically and emotionally healthy adults, and educators can focus on teaching.
- Ensure that no child's future is determined by their zip code, parents' income, race, or disability.
- Provide every middle and high school student a path to a successful career. Start investing in our children at birth.[2]

Every Democratic candidate in the field supports some variation of universal health care. Joe Biden supports "health insurance as a right—not a privilege," which he proposes to achieve by expanding upon the popular parts of the Affordable Healthcare Act.

The former vice president wants to "tackle" climate change and pollution, and to "ensure that every American has access to clean drinking water, clean air, and an environment free of pollutants." Biden will face a lot of campaign competition on climate change issues from candidates on his left flank. But *PolitiFact* rated his claim of being a climate change pioneer by introducing a bill to take action all the way back in 1987 as "True," which is a claim nobody else in the field will be able to make.[3]

The former chair of the Senate's judiciary committee lists "reforming our criminal justice system" as one of his top priorities for the middle class. His plans include taking action against gun violence, which his federal assault weapons ban in 1994 did achieve, and reauthorizing his crime bill's landmark Violence Against Women Act, which is expired as of the writing of this book. Biden's 1994 crime bill is not well looked upon today for its role in perfecting America's racially disparate system of mass incarceration, but Biden has been steadily working on sentencing reforms for a dozen years now, and would remain committed to that cause if elected.[4]

On marijuana issues, the entire Democratic 2020 field favors legalization, a major turn of events, but Biden favors a different approach: recategorizing the plant from a Schedule I drug listing down to a Schedule II drug.[5, 6] That would mean that the strict Food and Drug Administration would regulate cannabis. However, his spokesman also said Biden would let the states decide about marijuana legalization, so it may be too early to tell what his position would be, if elected.

Biden raged against the tax cuts at the start of this century and his platform seeks to reward work, "not just wealth." He defines that as stronger labor laws and "a tax code that rewards the middle class" but doesn't directly mention the hole blown in America's budget by the Trump tax cuts.

Next, Biden wants to ensure "our workers and communities benefit from international trade." That means better enforcement of existing trade laws and public investment in worker training. His website says that "we need to write the rules of the road for international trade through a modern, inclusive process," which doesn't mention the Trans-Pacific Partnership (TPP), a seven-year-long Obama-administration trade initiative that would've rewritten NAFTA for the modern era, as well as created a massive trading bloc to counter China's rising economic influence. Obama's trade deal was written mostly in secret, but when it finished, even Republican Speaker of the House Paul Ryan (R-WI) supported the TPP, but the head of his party, Donald Trump, killed it early in his administration.[7] A Biden trade deal would:

- Implement rules that protect our workers
- Safeguard the environment
- Uphold labor standards and middle-class wages
- Foster innovation
- Take on big global challenges like corporate concentration, corruption, and climate change.

In some ways, Biden's trade plans resemble the goals of the TPP.

Lastly, Joe Biden wants to strengthen America's middle class by "pursuing a humane immigration policy that upholds our values, strengthens our economy, and secures our border." That means addressing the "root causes of migration." His campaign website notes that "at the same time, we must never forget that immigration is the reason the United States has been able to constantly renew and reinvent itself."

Former Vice President Biden's plan to "demonstrate respected leadership on the world stage" is something he knows about implementing, because he was one of the Obama administration's key figures in righting the mistakes made by the George W. Bush administration, including handling two foreign wars. "America is strongest when we lead not only with the example of our power, but the power of our example," reads his campaign website.

His three-point foreign affairs agenda starts at home, with the subject of his evocative first campaign video: fighting a rising tide of hate and domestic terror in America. He calls "inclusivity, tolerance, diversity, respect for the rule of law, freedom of speech, freedom of the press, freedom of religion . . . the values that are the basis of our democracy." They are.

Biden wants to recommit to America's allies. Joe Biden is and has been a liberal internationalist throughout his career, and a proponent of the North Atlantic Treaty Organization (NATO), as well as America's traditionally close relationship with its European allies, the EU, Japan, and other liberal democracies throughout the world.

Joe Biden wants to use America's military power responsibly. That means modernizing our military and saving our firepower so that we only send troops "into harm's way" when it is in our vital national interest. Judging by the Obama administration's anti-interventionist stance, that would mean a more conservative use of the military abroad. However, Biden is sure to face questions about America's involvement in the Saudi Arabian and UAE war in Yemen, which began under Obama, but then vastly expanded under President Trump, who has cultivated an exceedingly close relationship with Riyadh.

Lastly, Biden's campaign vision is to make sure our democracy includes everyone. "Either all of us decide who runs and wins elected office," his campaign website states, "or only a few do." For the former vice president, that means protecting the right to vote and ending the dominance of big money in our democracy. America is facing down an epidemic of discriminatory laws and unethical public officials restricting the vote, which Biden compares to the south's old Jim Crow laws. On top of giving greater access to the ballot box, Biden is strongly in favor of protecting our democratic machinery from foreign powers who seek to undermine our political order, such as the Russian hackers who helped the Trump campaign win in 2016, a fact even Donald Trump admitted publicly at the end of May 2019.

Biden's plan to balance the playing field for political candidates who aren't rich like himself is to create a public financing system for federal campaigns and a constitutional amendment overturning the *Citizens United* decision by the Supreme Court, which threw the doors open to a flood of dark money and foreign meddling.

BIOGRAPHY: BIDEN'S METEORIC RISE TO OFFICE AND HIS FAMILY TRAGEDY

J oseph Robinette Biden Jr.'s road to the vice presidency began on November 20, 1942, when he was born the eldest son to parents living in working-class Scranton, Pennsylvania, where he spent his first ten years living in the Green Ridge neighborhood.[1] He and Senator Bernie Sanders—along with the current Democratic Speaker of the House Nancy Pelosi—are all members of the "silent generation" who were born before the end of World War II, unlike our current president, who is from the "baby boom" generation.[2]

Biden's meteoric rise from middle-class Scranton to the U.S. Senate was only interrupted by a crushing personal loss that left him a thirty-year-old widower and single father before he was even sworn into office. It's a story of tragedy and triumph that has defined the vice president's life, both personally and politically, ever since 1972.

Biden has lost two of his four children under devastating circumstances: a young daughter who perished, along with his first wife, in a car accident, and his eldest son's early demise to brain cancer at age forty-six. His surviving son, Hunter Biden, is a forty-nine-year-old Yale-educated attorney who runs a private equity firm. Joe Biden has been married to his second wife, schoolteacher Jill, since June 1977. His youngest daughter, Ashley Biden—his only child with Jill—is thirty-seven and holds a master's in social work from Penn, and served as the executive director of the Delaware Center for Justice until recently.[3, 4]

Young Joe was a daring child, fearless and an athlete, whose formative lessons in politics came in the heavily Democratic neighborhood where he spent his first decade, in the home of his grandparents.[5] "It was a neighborhood. It was a sense of togetherness. It was an ethic," Biden told the *Scranton Times-Tribune* in 2008 after earning the Democratic nomination for vice president. "The other thing [about Green Ridge] was to be Irish, was to be a Democrat, was to be a Catholic. There was no light between the three. . . It's not like that where I'm from [Delaware]."

Joe Biden's maternal great grandfather from Scranton was a Pennsylvania state senator who became one the first Irish Roman Catholics in public office in the state in 1907.[6] His "Grandfather Finnegan" became his political mentor on numerous weekend trips.[7] The *HuffPost* traced the Finnegan side of Biden's family tree all the way back to County Louth, Ireland, where amazingly, Biden's ancestors from Ireland had the same profession—shoemakers—as did President Obama's Irish ancestry. Both men's progenitors also arrived in the spring of 1849 toward the end of the Great Potato Famine.

His father, Joe Biden, Sr., had been wealthy early in life, but experienced deep financial setbacks by the time his eldest son was born, the first of his four children with Catherine Eugenia Biden (née Finnegan). His mother's Irish family sheltered the Biden family in Scranton when times were tough as the town's coal mines and garment mills closed and jobs became scarce. Joe Sr. had lived an early life of privilege—for example, sailing yachts off the New England coast in his twenties—but wound up forced to move into a crowded two-bedroom apartment in Claymont, Delaware, nearby Wilmington, which is why the former vice president came of age there. Joe Sr. became a used-car salesman in Delaware, and his son grew up to become a top high school athlete. His football coach John Walsh called Biden "the most talented receiver I ever had" at Archmere, where he caught the game-winning pass to cap an undefeated season, graduating in 1961.[8] Toward the end of his days at Archmere High School, he attended a sit-in against a segregated theater.

"My dad always said, 'Champ, the measure of a man is not how often he is knocked down, but how quickly he gets up,'" said Biden to the *New York Times*. "I've never seen a time in my career when so many Americans have been knocked down." Later, the *New York Times* described a 2008 campaign appearance where Biden's voice rose, his face reddening beneath his "thin crown of white hair" as he delivered the stirring conclusion at an appearance in Rochester, New Hampshire.[9] "As my father used to say, when you get knocked down, get up!" Joe Sr. passed away in 2002, at the ripe old age of eighty-six.

Joe Biden continued on to college at the University of Delaware, from which he graduated with a double major in history and political science in 1965.[10] As a junior, he flew to the Bahamas for spring break where he met the woman who would change his life forever, Neilia Hunter.[11] Her family owned diners in upstate New York, and the ambitious young Joe told

Neilia's mother that his career plan was to be president of the United States. It was "love at first sight."[12]

After graduating from college, Biden immediately enrolled in Syracuse University's law school in the spring of 1965, and graduated three years later. However, he was not the world's greatest student, placing seventy-sixth in a class of eighty-five and nearly getting kicked out of school for behavior that was admittedly a "dangerous combination of arrogant and sloppy." Biden had used five pages of a law review article without proper credit, and he later admitted that he "hadn't been to class enough to know how to do citations." It was an incident that would later haunt his 1988 presidential campaign.

Neilia Hunter and Joe Biden were married on August 27, 1966, after he finished the grueling first year of law school, a "weeding-out" year in which students are known as 1L's and known for encyclopedic study habits. Two years later, Biden graduated from law school and went into private practice as a trial attorney living in the suburbs of Wilmington, Delaware; he served as a public defender. A year after that, his eldest son Joseph R. "Beau" Biden III was born on February 3, 1969, and his brother Hunter followed one year and a day later. Nine months after his second son was born, Biden won his first election, to Delaware's New Castle County Council on November 8, 1970. The following year, Biden started his own law firm, and his wife Neilia gave birth to his third child, a daughter named Naomi. As his family expanded, the ambitious young attorney's political star rose as well, and culminated in an electoral splash at the age of twenty-nine, when Joe Biden improbably defeated the Republican Senator J. Caleb Boggs by just 3,126 votes while almost weeks shy of thirty-years-old, the minimum age to serve. Boggs was a Delaware institution who had also served as the state's U.S. representative and governor during his long career.

Biden entered the race against Sen. Boggs as a true underdog when no other Democrat wanted to challenge the longtime incumbent. He hired pollster Patrick Caddell and consultant John Marttila for that race, and the two men continued to serve the senator for many years afterward.[13] His campaign assistant, Ted Kaufman, then an employee of DuPont, said he didn't have a chance, and later went on to be his chief of staff and eventually his senate successor from 2009 to 2010.

Joe Sr. campaigned door-to-door for his son. The candidate's sister, Valerie Biden Owen—a schoolteacher like his wife Nelia—ran that campaign and subsequent ones. She recalled to NPR that they distributed thousands of printed "newspapers" with her brother's campaign positions.[14] Biden's sister called that first campaign "a children's crusade because of its many youthful volunteers." It was Biden's anti-war stance against Vietnam, his messaging about civil rights, and his desire for change that stirred voters' passions, all of which the young lawyer highlighted in contrast with the aging Republican incumbent. Still, the sixty-three-year-old Sen. Boggs had 93 percent recognition across the state, and Biden had only 18 percent.[15]

On Tuesday, November 7, 1972, the state of Delaware voted for President Nixon, the Republican incumbent president, by over twenty points.[16] Joe Biden defeated J. Caleb Boggs by a margin of 50.5 percent to 49.1 percent of the vote.[17] "I can remember the thought as if it was yesterday," Kaufman told NPR in late 2007, during the senator's second presidential campaign. "I will never again think of something as impossible."[18] Thirteen days later, Senator-elect Biden turned thirty and advanced his preparations to begin his new job in Washington, DC, working there throughout the holiday season. His wife Neilia was the "brains" behind his campaign and his "top advisor."[19] Media comparisons between Biden and former President John F. Kennedy started during the campaign and intensified after his upset win.

EARLY SENATE CAREER

Joe Biden's senatorial career lasted longer than all but sixteen others out of the 1,982 other men and women to serve in the upper chamber of Congress. His ideological leanings varied over the course of his thirty-six years in office. But his Vote View ratings and a look at key moments show that he was always in the mainstream of his party, maintaining a voting record in lockstep with the Senate Democratic Caucus roughly 80 percent of the time over the course of his career.[1]

Senator Biden's ideology was middle of the pack for Democrats, though liberal in comparison to the Senate as a whole.[2] He broke with his party on social issues, but also got many Republican senators to break with their party on his policy priorities to craft bipartisan solutions. As a politician who first represents his constituents, Biden's ideology has moved issue by issue from his most liberal voting record in the late 1980s as he geared up for his first presidential bid to its most conservative run in 1997. That's when his voting record was only slightly to the right of current Senator Patrick Leahy (D-VT), his longtime colleague on the judiciary committee.[3]

"He seems drawn again and again to try to reconcile the economic and cultural liberalism of the national Democratic Party, of which he is one of the leaders, with the economic and cultural conservatism of so many of those he grew up with: to explain one to the other, to reconcile them, to enable them to live happily together," reported PolitiFact about Biden's profile in the 1996 *Almanac of American Politics*. "During Biden's time in the Senate, just over 40 percent of the bills he co-sponsored were introduced by Republicans, according to an analysis by Benjamin Hammer of GovTrack."

THE THIRTY-YEAR-OLD SENATOR-ELECT'S PERSONAL TRAGEDIES

"It's too perfect," Biden later recalled his feelings after first getting elected to the senate in a *Politico* interview. "[It] can't be like this. Something's gonna happen." He sadly was correct; tragedy didn't wait long to strike the Biden family after that election.[4] On the night of December 17, 1972, Neilia Biden loaded her three children into the family car to go buy a Christmas tree. She crossed a rural intersection with a two-way stop and her car was broadsided by a tractor trailer carrying corncobs; it happened during a bygone era of cars without seat belts, let alone mandatory child safety seats. Neilia was carrying the one-year-old baby Naomi on her lap, and neither of them survived the accident; Beau made it, and so did Hunter, the former with a crushed pelvis and the latter with a crushed skull.[5] Even President Nixon called the young senator-elect to give his condolences, a call which was captured by the White House tape recording system and later released.

Senator-elect Biden had to be coaxed into taking the oath of office by Democratic minority leader Mike Mansfield (D-MT), who asked him to give the office at least six months.[6] The senate brought his swearing-in ceremony to Beau and Hunter's hospital room in Wilmington, Delaware, on January 3, 1973.[7] He became the sixth-youngest senator ever sworn in.[8]

Senate Majority Whip Robert C. Byrd (D-VW) was the only member of Congress to attend the funeral.[9]

But it was a bleak, grief-stricken term.

What Joe Biden learned from losing half of his family is something intangible that has defined his political career ever since: empathy. As vice president in 2012, he later told an audience of veterans on Memorial Day that, "for the first time in my life, I understood how someone could consciously decide to commit suicide. Not because they were deranged, not because they were nuts, because they'd been to the top of the mountain and they just knew in their heart they'd never get there again, that it was . . . never going to be that way ever again."[10]

A senior Democratic senator—John McClellan of Arkansas—told Biden to bury himself in work, which he did, with a 90 percent attendance record that year.[11] His sister Valerie moved in with him for the next four years. And that's when the young senator began taking the ninety-minutes-each-way daily commute on Amtrak from Wilmington to DC and back, that would eventually become part of his political legend (and lead to the Wilmington station being named after him). Even after losing his beloved Neilia, Biden retained presidential ambitions, though he declined most of the flood of early media requests seeking to tell the story of his star-crossed marriage. He did give an in-depth interview to journalist Kitty Kelley, who later became famous for her tell-all unauthorized biographies, and her journalistic errors. She wrote in the *Washingtonian*:

> *In his office in the New Senate Office Building surrounded by more than 35 pictures of his late wife, Biden*

launched into a three-hour reminiscence. It wasn't maudlin—he seemed to enjoy remembering aloud. He was the handsome football hero. She was the beautiful homecoming queen. Their marriage was perfect. Their children were beautiful. And they almost lived happily ever after. "Neilia was my very best friend, my greatest ally, my sensuous lover. The longer we lived together the more we enjoyed everything from sex to sports. Most guys don't really know what I lost because they never knew what I had. Our marriage was sensational. It was exceptional, and now that I look around at my friends and my colleagues, I know more than ever how phenomenal it really was. When you lose something like that, you lose a part of yourself that you never get back again.

Some detractors accuse him of shrouding himself in widower's weeds, of dredging up his late wife in every speech. But Biden prides himself on being candid and honest—"That's the only way I could be with the wife I had." He understands the accusations: "I'm not the kind of guy everyone likes. My personality either grabs you or it doesn't. My sister says I almost lost the campaign because of my personality, and my brother-in-law says you either love me or you hate me. I'm not an in-between type."[12]

Kelley's story inaccurately portrayed a joke Biden told two other senators in an elevator—requiring a correction—but the interview is replete with reminders that America was still a man's world in 1974.[13] Still, her interview is a fair snapshot of Joe Biden in June 1974, just before the turmoil of Watergate engulfed America's political center of gravity and led to the first ever presidential resignation from office.

Senator Biden was not part of the Watergate Committee, nor are there any stories about his role in the investigations that ultimately led the House judiciary committee to vote to impeach the president, leading to Nixon's resignation. However, he did make poignant remarks about the presidential resignation on the Senate floor on the one-month anniversary, because, "this Watergate affair leaves us—at least me—with the uncomfortable feeling that this is still more a government of men than of laws." He later continued, describing the kind of president that America needs:

The Office of Presidency has come a long way from the three clerks of the Washington administration and the time when Thomas Jefferson conducted official business in the boarding-house parlor off his bedroom.

Presidents have come to be looked upon-and have looked upon themselves-as war-and-peace makers, mythmakers, and rainmakers. Men of learning, who should know better, have assisted at these creations. The time has come for Presidents to promise not more, but less. The time has come for Americans to elect as Presidents those who, as they toil, are competent, accessible, fair-dealing, plain-speaking persons willing to share their burdens—and glory—with the Congress.

> *Presidents are needed to render unto the Congress the things that are Congress's—for example, a full role in the war powers and a full role in budgetary policy. These traits would be their distinctions. I do not believe these are Sunday sentiments to be ignored on legislative days. These observations are not theory. We are confronted, in fact, with a condition not a theory. Three consecutive Presidents have been unexpectedly removed from office—the first by assassination, the second by forced retirement and the third, just one month ago, by forced resignation. We, in the Congress, had better abandon our Presidential crutches and look to ourselves for a full role in governing.[14]*

Biden's words from forty-five years ago resonate even more so today, during the Trump administration. He concluded by listing nine ideas for post-Watergate reforms, including the idea that all of Congress' proceedings be televised, a dream that only became reality due to the privately run C-SPAN network.

The young widower also met the woman to whom he is still married today in 1975, when his brother set him up on a blind date with Jill Tracy Jacobs.[15] It turned out that Joe had seen Jill's picture in a local advertisement, and they hit it off. On June 17, 1977, the couple wed in a private ceremony at the United Nations Chapel in New York City. Hunter and Beau Biden joined them at the ceremony, and on the honeymoon. He surprised his Senate staff by telling them about his wedding only the day before.[16] Six years later, their only daughter, Ashley, was born. His happy second marriage became a storybook ending for Biden, but it happened during turbulent times in America with rising crime and racial tension in the north spilling into the streets.

FROM PRO-BUSING TO ANTIBUSING

Some of Joe Biden's political positions from the 1970s have reemerged as out of step with the Democratic Party's modern values, but as the *Los Angeles Times*'s Janet Hook writes, they don't define his positions forty years later:

> Many of Biden's positions were well within the mainstream of the Democratic Party at the time he took them. But the party is now far more sensitive to discrimination against gays, sexual harassment and racial inequality than when Biden first came to Washington. The capital has changed, too. The Senate Biden entered as a 30-year-old in 1973 was still a bastion of bipartisan backslapping, where compromise was not a dirty word. The Democratic Party was a coalition of Southern conservatives and Northern liberals. Liberal Republicans were still a thriving political faction.

The senator from Delaware supported school busing to effect racial integration during his 1972 campaign, but soon afterward found out the sting of angry constituents against the plan. Racial violence was erupting in the

Northeast at that time, especially in Boston, when northern states who supported the Civil Rights Act didn't want to implement the law. Even busing advocates admitted that it wasn't an ideal solution to desegregate schools, but there wasn't and still today aren't a lot of good alternative ideas to increase racial integration in schools.

Wilmington's school system was placed under a court order to desegregate in 1974. That's when a group of vehemently antibusing residents held a stinging meeting that June at a school in its suburbs, specifically to rebuke the senator for his early votes in favor of his position which supported legislative compromises to maintain the practice of busing. Biden explained his nuanced position that he was against "de jure" segregation or racist policies and not "de facto" segregated schools which happened due to neighborhoods being racially segregated. "We're going to hound Biden for the next four years if he doesn't vote our position," replied the leader of the demonstration.[17]

The following year, Biden supported an amendment to end busing to effect desegregation in schools put forth by conservative southern GOP Senator Jesse Helms, and ultimately got his own antibusing amendment pushed through the senate.[18] He also supported an antibusing amendment submitted by Sen. Byrd. It was a 180-degree turn for Biden, who argued then that African Americans didn't want to be desegregated for reasons of "black pride."[19] At the time, journalists asked Biden if he was still a liberal in light of his busing stance, and he replied:

> It is true that the white man has suppressed the black man, and continues to suppress the black man. It is

*harder to be black than to be white. But you have to open
up avenues for blacks without closing avenues for whites;
you don't hold society back to let one segment catch up.
You put more money into the black schools for remedial
reading programs, you upgrade facilities, you upgrade
opportunities, open up housing patterns. You give every-
body a piece of the action.*[20]

To his credit, when Wilmington's schools were finally integrated through busing in 1976, he told students, "You shouldn't hate black kids," according to the Delaware *Evening Journal*.[21] "We disagreed on busing," says former executive director of the Leadership Conference on Civil Rights, Ralph G. Neas, in a recent *Post* story about Biden's positions in the 1970s, "but I always looked to Biden as a leader in the field of civil rights in other critical areas."[22]

That year, Senator Biden became one of eventual President Jimmy Carter's earliest endorsements during the 1976 Democratic primary, and continued supporting him even when fellow Senator Ted Kennedy mounted a primary challenge four years later.[23] He won reelection by sixteen points in 1978, but the first African American member of the Senate from Massachusetts who supported busing lost.

EXPANDING RESPONSIBILITY THROUGH COMMITTEE LEADERSHIP

Joe Biden's work chairing senate committees grew to be one of the defining components of his thirty-six year tenure in Congress.

In January 1975, Biden was named to the Senate Committee on Foreign Relations, which he would eventually chair from 2001 to 2003 and from 2007 to 2009.[24] Two years later, the Delaware senator would be named to the Committee on the Judiciary. He became the ranking member of the Senate judiciary committee in 1981 and, consequently, its chair from 1987 until 1994.

Senator Biden became a member of the newly formed Senate Select Committee on Intelligence, founded in 1976 after the Church Committee revealed mass domestic surveillance programs and other major abuses by the CIA.[25] He formed a subcommittee on secrecy and grappled with the balance between intelligence agencies disclosing national security information and what happens if they mislead Congress.[26] The issue became a very real problem after the CIA director pled guilty to lying to Congress that year. Four years later, Biden would be responsible for legislation that narrowed the penalties for revealing the names of U.S. intelligence agents to protect the press's First Amendment rights to report on national security matters.[27]

As a member of the foreign relations panel, Biden established himself as a "liberal internationalist" and was heavily involved in the 1970s nuclear arms control treaties known as Strategic Arms Limitation Treaties (SALT) with the former Soviet Union.[28] He also argued against developing the Reagan administration's Strategic Defense Initiative, derisively nicknamed "Star Wars" by Senate Democrats, which would've violated the SALT agreements. Reagan's SDI program turned into an expensive flop.[29]

After a widely condemned speech by President Reagan in 1986 that many saw as soft-pedaling South Africa's racist apartheid state, the senator from Delaware "blistered" his Secretary of State George Shultz for the administration's lackluster efforts there, railing against their refusal to act on a "morally abhorrent" policy.[30, 31]

However, Senator Biden's most lasting legislative legacy—for better or worse—has been shaped by his time on the Senate judiciary committee. He "ignored advice to be more partisan" and cultivated a close relationship with former "Dixiecrat" and 1948 segregationist presidential candidate Senator Strom Thurmond (R-SC).[32] Thurmond chaired the judiciary committee and nothing legislative would happen without his support. Biden used that relationship to shape national policy. First, he coined the term "drug czar" in 1982, and helped create the position as a cabinet office.[33] Then, he shepherded the Crime Control Act of 1984 into law, moving it through his committee in bipartisan fashion.[34] It was the first major revision of the federal criminal code in eight decades, established the U.S. Sentencing Commission to create federal guidelines that bring national consistency in criminal sentencing.[35] The Crime Control Act also instituted more serious penalties for gun crimes. But it also reinstituted the federal death penalty—only used three times since then, with sixty-three federal death row inmates today. And it established the federal asset forfeiture law known as "equitable sharing" that was abused by law enforcement, as well as amping up criminal sentences in the "War on Drugs," which is only winding down today.

In 1986, Senator Biden achieved one of his signature results in the judiciary committee by denying a federal judgeship to an Alabama U.S. attorney named Jefferson Beauregard Sessions III over his racist biases. It would become only the second time in forty-eight years that a federal judge appointee lost a confirmation vote.[36] Sessions later went on to become a senator, then an early supporter of President Trump and eventually his first attorney general.

Although, the result of Biden's dispatching Sessions's judicial nomination wasn't the same as denying a lifetime seat on the Supreme Court, it was a major achievement for the ranking member to sidetrack a nomination across party lines. While it wasn't equivalent to the hearings about Judge Brett Kavanaugh, it was politically significant in a midterm election year when nearly two dozen Republican Senate seats were up for grabs while they held a slim majority, similar in numbers to the 2020 general election's senate race map.

"Joe reached a point in his career where he faced a political ultimatum: You either lead the charge or get run over by it," a Republican Senate aide told the *Washington Post* that year. "He became more hard-nosed, more intransigent."[37] Democrats would gain eight seats that year to flip the Senate blue.[38] It became an open secret that Biden was eyeing a presidential campaign when Reagan left office.

The following year would become the defining moment of the middle of Senator Biden's career. He began a Democratic primary campaign and simultaneously oversaw the first of two controversial Supreme Court nominations by Republican presidents as the chairman of the Senate judiciary committee.

SENATOR BIDEN'S FIRST PRESIDENTIAL RUN AND THE BORK HEARINGS

Senator Joe Biden's national political career truly began in earnest when he took the helm of the prestigious Senate Committee on the Judiciary, and launched a bid for the 1988 Democratic nomination for president. But just as Biden's campaign was beginning to gain early traction in Iowa and on the eve of his nationally televised role overseeing the Supreme Court nomination of Robert Bork—in which he succeeded tremendously in the Senate—his promising presidential campaign would ingloriously collapse under the weight of his duties and damaging revelations.

Yet, Senator Biden persisted throughout the roller-coaster ride of the primary and the hearings, even burnishing his credentials inside the DC Beltway for making shrewd decisions throughout, and demonstrating grace and humility. Forced to choose between a struggling presidential campaign and a supportive Senate beckoning him to finish presiding over Judge Bork's nomination, Biden chose to prioritize doing his job in the judiciary committee.

In the end, Joe Biden achieved something more important for the country than any political race. He restored the Senate's role in advising the White House on judicial nominees, and he helped prevent the Supreme Court from taking a far-right turn for thirty years, a situation Democrats have only begun to confront in the wake of President Trump's election to office.

Both Biden and Senator Gary Hart (D-CO) left the 1988 Democratic primary, but only one of them survived the experience. In the Delaware senator's instance, it was more than a metaphorical survival, but a medical fight for his life, that concluded a defining year in Joe Biden's career.

AN AUSPICIOUS LATE START TO THE CAMPAIGN

Joe Biden launched his campaign for the 1988 Democratic primary nomination to replace term-limited President Ronald Reagan on June 10, 1987. There were twenty-two family members in attendance that day at the Wilmington, Delaware, train station that now bears his name. At the age of forty-four, he had to juggle the high-profile chairmanship and a national political campaign. In the *New York Times*, E.J. Dionne described the scene:

> Pledging that he would challenge Americans to rise above "the mere accumulation of material things," Senator Joseph R. Biden Jr. today announced his candidacy for the Democratic nomination for President. "For too long in this society, we have celebrated unrestrained individualism over common community," Mr. Biden declared in

this city where he made his political start as a county councilman. "For too long as a nation, we have been lulled by the anthem of self-interest," he continued.

"For a decade, led by Ronald Reagan, self-aggrandizement has been the full-throated cry of this society: 'I've got mine so why don't you get yours' and 'What's in it for me?' . . . We must rekindle the fire of idealism in our society," he said in language that recalled the speeches of John F. Kennedy, "for nothing suffocates the promise of America more than unbounded cynicism and indifference."[1]

Joe Biden had $2 million in the bank at the time, equivalent to $4.2 million in 2019 dollars. However well regarded he was inside of politics, he was only polling at 1 to 3 percent at the time, sixth out of eight candidates. Dionne noted that the senator was staking his campaign on his oratorical prowess and his high-profile chairmanship, not his legislative record, as he advocated for generational change in that election. He was seeking to replace the oldest president in American history to that date in that race.

BIDEN OVERSEES JUDICIARY COMMITTEE WHEN A KEY SUPREME COURT SEAT BECOMES VACANT

Two and a half weeks later, Supreme Court Justice Lewis F. Powell, Jr. announced his retirement after fifteen years on the bench.[2] He was the key moderate swing vote on the court, and the Reagan administration viewed his replacement as an opportunity to turn the top court in a conservative direction for years to come. Then-Democratic Senate Majority Leader Robert Byrd (D-WV) publicly warned the White House not to select the DC circuit court judge Robert H. Bork for the position, but a day later Reagan submitted his nomination to the high court.[3, 4] Senator Ted Kennedy (D-MA) didn't waste any time calling his views on the constitution "extremist" and "Neanderthal." Furthermore, Bork held a prominent role in Watergate as Nixon's hatchet man in the infamous Saturday Night Massacre; he was the solicitor general then, but after the president fired his superiors, he illegally and arbitrarily wiped out Department of Justice regulations to fire special prosecutor Archibald Cox.[5]

In early August 1987, Biden scheduled ten days of hearings for the following month to run concurrently with hearings on new FBI Director nominee William Sessions.[6] By then, the primary campaign was in full swing and the national media took note of the Delaware senator's dual role as both candidate and chairman after an August 23rd primary debate at the Iowa State Fair. Many believed that opposing Bork and failing to sway his Senate colleagues could doom his presidential bid, and it was undeniable that the proceeding was taking him off the summer campaign trail in Iowa.[7] Senator Biden floated being open to Bork's rise to the Supreme Court during the prior election year, and didn't take an immediate stance on Bork's nomination partly because he had to balance his duties running the process with his own stance.

His solution was to go beyond politics and focus Bork's nomination to be about the facts, so the senator hired researchers to prepare a seventy-five-page dossier on Bork called the "Biden Report," which he released the Thursday before Labor Day, barely two weeks before the hearing began. The *Los Angeles Times* reported:

> Prepared by consultants to Sen. Joseph R. Biden Jr. (D-Del.), said a White House "briefing book" on Bork, which paints him as a moderate judge of the "mainstream tradition," is a "distortion of his record" and contains "major inaccuracies." Biden, a Democratic presidential candidate, commissioned the report to counter the White House paper, written to soften Bork's image as a hardline conservative. The Administration is promoting Bork as a moderate like Justice Lewis F. Powell Jr., whom he was nominated to replace.
>
> Biden's consultants, Washington lawyer Jeffrey Peck and Duke University law professor Christopher Schroeder, concluded that Bork is not an advocate of judicial restraint, as the White House claims, but actually is a judicial activist determined to advance President Reagan's conservative social agenda well into the next century.
>
> "From his record, it appears that Bork's addition to the court would cement a five-vote majority for undoing much of the social progress of the last three decades," they wrote. "An accurate portrait of Judge Bork's record leaves no doubt that he has been a conservative activist and not a practitioner of judicial restraint."[8]

The Senate required sixty votes to end debate in order to hold a vote to confirm Bork's nomination to the high court, Democrats controlled fifty-four of those votes. The Biden Report was a shot across the bow to the Reagan administration that the former Nixon official was going to have a hard time winning over those votes. (In 2017, Republican Senate Majority leader Mitch McConnell lowered the threshold to fifty votes for Supreme Court nominees, which he calls the "nuclear option.")

A MEDIA FIRESTORM

Then something unexpected happened when a major negative report by Maureen Dowd about Biden's recent debate speech appeared on the front page of the *New York Times* just below the fold, at a time when page placement of stories was very important for their visibility and impact.[9] Dowd revealed that Joe Biden frequently quoted the United Kingdom's Labour Party opposition leader Neil Kinnock on the trail, but that, at the debate, he had recounted a story about being the first in his family to attend college, telling the audience that the thought had actually occurred to him on the ride to a fairground. In fact, Biden had adapted—without attribution—part of a recent, successful ten-minute-long speech by Kinnock broadcast on the BBC.

The impact on his campaign wasn't immediately devastating, but it raised key questions about Biden's credibility as an oratorical candidate. The timing couldn't have been worse, landing just a few days before the media universe descended on Washington, DC, for the politically charged Bork nomination hearings. He and his campaign immediately responded to the Associated Press that omitting attribution to Kinnock was accidental, and cast aspersion on the other Democratic campaigns for allegedly disseminating the videos on the eve of the Bork hearings.[10] The following day, Biden's campaign pushed back hard against the story, saying that criticism came with the territory, and lamenting the impact of intraparty warfare on really important proceedings in DC. His press secretary told the AP's Carolyn Skorneck that Dowd's story didn't have "a whit of impact," and it wouldn't derail the campaign.[11, 12]

At that moment, they were right: regional news outlets were more focused on the Bork hearings and not Biden's political gaffe. "I wish we had something like that," said another Democratic campaign adviser, Sergio Bendixen, discussing the national spotlight Senator Biden would command directing Bork's questioning, to a young John Harwood—who is now CNBC's lead political reporter—at the *St. Petersburg Times*.[13]

That day, the highly anticipated Bork hearings began, and the national Knight-Ridder newspaper chain dug up another instance of Biden using another politician's words in his speech to the California Democratic Party convention, without direct attribution to the audience, just to reporters.[14] Then, the next day, a major revelation landed when Biden's trip to the disciplinary board at Syracuse Law School surfaced in the *New York Times*.[15] The following day, Biden admitted his mistake, which he said was not "malevolent" and released a sixty-five-page file of his law school records to the *New York Times*, which had the negative side effect of telling readers that he was at the bottom of his class.[16] He wasn't severely penalized by the school, which could've expelled him for a more serious offense. But the damage was being done one cut at a time with the continuing media coverage.

A BIPARTISAN GROUP OF SENATORS RALLIES AROUND BIDEN

A bipartisan group of senators rallied around the embattled Senator Biden, who was methodically managing the questioning of Judge Bork in the nationally televised hearings. "I don't know where all this stuff will go with regard to your present situation," said Alan Simpson, the Republican senator from Wyoming, to the *New York Times* in a reference to Teddy Roosevelt.[17] "Hang on tight. You have at least had the guts to throw yourself in the public arena, to run for the Presidency. And that's better than a lot of faint-hearted detractors will ever do in this world, and they will be the ones who will try to sully you and pull you down." The Democratic Senate Majority leader Byrd also offered words of public support to Biden as a man of good intentions, "whose credibility is good with me."

Even Senator Orrin Hatch (R-UT), Bork's greatest ally, complimented Biden's handling of the judiciary committee hearings, saying he got a "bad rap" on his speeches. Ranking member Sen. Thurmond also defended Biden, telling the *Washington Post* that he wanted the Delaware senator to "stay on" and that, "I expressed my support. And nobody expressed their opinion to the contrary. I took that to be pretty solid support." Such a public expression of bipartisan support is nonexistent in today's Washington, DC, environment, let alone in support of a presidential candidate of the opposite party who is struggling with a growing scandal during a nationally relevant partisan political showdown. He cast himself as just a "regular guy" with regular-guy flaws, but the explanations, apologies, and disclosures fanned the flames of negative publicity along the lines of the political truism attributed to President Reagan and former Rep. J. C. Watts: "If you're explaining, you're losing."

JOE BIDEN ★ 63

That's when the Bork hearings took a dramatic turn in Biden's favor, when Sen. Kennedy produced a fateful audio recording of the judge answering questions at the small Jesuit school Canisius College in Buffalo, New York. Robert Bork could be heard saying that "precedent doesn't matter." It was a dramatic end of the week, and more devastating to the judge's long-term reputation than anything that happened to Biden because of his gaffes. The Delaware senator used his role as chairman to publicly chide Bork, saying he "worries the devil" out of people, for refusing to admit that American women have a right to privacy or the right to control their own bodies and get an abortion if they choose.[18]

BIDEN'S CAMPAIGN ENDS AMID "EXAGGERATED SHADOW" OF PAST MISDEEDS

The following Monday morning, Associated Press reporter Evans Witt broke a bombshell story that would prove to be terminal for Biden's campaign.[19] He had told a New Hampshire audience that he finished in the top half of his law school class in a video captured by C-SPAN and that, "I think I probably have a much higher IQ than you do," before claiming falsely that he got a full scholarship to the school (he only got a half scholarship) and that he progressed academically (he didn't) and that he won awards as an undergraduate (he didn't). Witt also revealed the source of the law school information, a former Dean of the school to whom Biden had written a letter requesting confidentiality, who let slip that problems were in the senator's file at a dinner with friends, one of whom contacted a reporter.

The fallout from Biden's departure was immediate, but didn't land inside the Senate. Ironically, his fellow senator from Colorado, Gary Hart, had pushed to take power out of the hands of the party, then lamented his own campaign's demise after an alleged extramarital affair was exposed by the *Miami Herald*. His exit signaled a major shift of power from party bosses, who had traditionally vetted candidates, to the media, and Hart became the second major Democratic nominee to drop out after a media firestorm the year before votes were counted.[20] While Hart's career in public service completely flamed out after he decried the media as hunters and candidates as the hunted, Senator Biden made a dignified exit, bemoaning the "exaggerated shadow" of his misdeeds. Wisely, Biden chose prioritizing the integrity of the continuing Bork nomination hearings according to a news analysis story by the AP's senior political reporter about Democrats fear of a longer political shadow from the two top candidates' failed campaigns:

> Rather than denounce those who reported the facts that undid his candidacy, Biden bowed out with some grace. "I'm angry with myself for having been put in the position—put myself in the position—of having to make this choice," said Biden. "And I am no less frustrated at the environment of presidential politics that makes it so difficult to let the American people measure the whole Joe Biden and not just misstatements that I have made."
>
> He looked at the assembled reporters and said, "You

warned me what it was going to be like. I thought I knew. It's a tough arena. And I'm a big boy. Sometimes you win, sometimes you lose. But now it's time for me to do just what I would have done had I not won in Iowa and just what I would have done had I lost on the convention floor. It's time for me to assess my mistakes and make sure that I don't make them again."

It also was a time for the Delaware senator to decide how to make certain he would survive the incident. It was not only his future in the 1988 presidential race that was threatened. To continue and keep the plagiarism issue alive might have threatened his future in the Senate. He must run for re-election in 1990 and could face a challenge from Republican Gov. Michael Castle.

So Biden moved quickly and managed to leave open the possibility he was right when he said, "There'll be other presidential campaigns, and I'll be there. There will be other opportunities, there'll be other battles in other places, other times, and I'll be there."[21]

Little did Biden know that there would be two more presidential campaigns in his future. But Biden did know that his position in the Senate would be safe. In fact, two years later, his Republican opponent would spend $75,000—the equivalent of $144,000 today—to mail out videotapes of his speech slipup, but still lost to Biden by over twenty points.[22, 23]

FINISHING THE BORK HEARINGS

In the *New York Times*, Senator Biden told Dionne that his new goal was to defeat the Bork nomination, and the reporter noted that the young senator was finally achieving the kind of broad respect from Washington's professionals that he had always sought.[24] "By removing himself from the Presidential contest on a conciliatory note," wrote Dionne, who has since become a syndicated columnist for the *Washington Post*, "Mr. Biden believed he had begun the task of reestablishing himself as 'a classy, strong man who definitely has a future in American politics,' said Thomas E. Donilon, a key adviser." Donilon went on to be the Obama administration's second National Security Advisor.

One week later at the end of September 1987, Bork's grueling twelve-day-long nomination hearings concluded. That is when former President Jimmy Carter decided to send his longtime political ally, Chairman Biden, a scathing letter about Bork, instructing him to vote against the judge's attempt to sell a revisionist history of himself, and against his civil rights positions, which Carter viewed as disqualifying Bork to sit on the Supreme Court.[25] It was front-page news. That same day, Gov. Michael Dukakis (D-MA)—who went on to be the Democratic nominee, but lost after a GOP smear campaign—accepted the resignation of his campaign manager and national political director for releasing the tapes that sunk Biden's campaign.[26] "It takes the sleaze issue away from us," said one anonymous surviving 1988 Democratic primary campaign manager to the *Washington Post,* about giving the Republican party a moral high ground politically.[27] "And that hurts." Dukakis went on to lose to President George H. W. Bush in the general election after the Republican lashed out with a racially provocative ad campaign portraying him as weak on crime.[28]

A week later, the Senate judiciary committee voted 9–5 against Bork's nomination, shocking the Reagan White House, who had hoped that Democratic Senator Howell Heflin—a former Chief Justice of the Alabama Supreme Court—would side with them and rally other more conservative Southern Democrats behind the nomination.[29] Republican Senator Arlen Specter also voted against Bork. Soon afterward, the Associated Press ran a story with their "whip count" of the eighty-nine senators who had declared their intentions to vote for or against Robert Bork's nomination. Needing sixty votes, Bork was twenty-four short, with four liberal Republican senators from the northeast and one from Oregon crossing party lines, along with two Democrats from Oklahoma and South Carolina in favor of the far-right-wing judge.[30]

Two weeks later, the Senate did something we rarely see today: they held an open floor debate on the Bork nomination. What was a novelty back then about the debate held on October 21, 1987, was that the speeches were all broadcast live on television and dominated the evening newscasts. Democratic senators had been openly advising Bork to drop his nomination, and both sides made passionate speeches over the course of seven hours.

Biden "charged that Bork's judicial philosophy 'risks dangerous consequences.' He accused Reagan of playing politics with the Bork nomination, and of seeking to place 'ideological allies' on the nation's federal courts," according to the AP, whose headline said that Judge Bork's Supreme Court nomination had no chance of winning confirmation.[31]

Two days later, the Bork nomination succumbed to the worst ever up-or-down floor vote, out of the eleven losing floor battles for confirmation to the Supreme Court to that date, losing 58–42.[32] A simple majority would've placed him on the high court. In contrast, the conservative jurist Antonin Scalia was approved for a Supreme Court seat by the Senate unanimously just a year earlier, with only a one-day hearing. It was a crushing blow for Reagan, late in his second term and embattled by Congress's public hearings during the Iran-Contra investigation.

Senator Biden was the very public face of opposition to Bork's nomination, and while he wasn't going to be president, he did reach the zenith of his powers as a lawmaker. But Republicans were not happy. The AP reported that although Bork wasn't the first nominee voted down on the floor, the result could have lasting consequences. The Senate Republican Conference was outraged in defeat, including their future leader:

> "We may waltz around this Maypole one more time," predicted Sen. Mitch McConnell, R-Ky., a Bork supporter who said the president's substitute nominee likely will be "a philosophical soulmate of Judge Bork." McConnell, although saying he would prefer to consider only a nominee's competence, achievement, integrity and temperament, contended that the Bork fight proves "the temptation to go for the political raw meat is just too great."
>
> "I will treat judicial philosophy as relevant and adopt the new standard established in this proceeding, and will apply it prospectively," McConnell said. Other senators

voiced concern over what McConnell called a "new Senate rule."[33]

Senator Biden's floor speech after Watergate talked about the president restoring to Congress what was its territory. In this case, the lame duck White House ate crow and sent Reagan's Chief of Staff Howard Baker to meet with Senate Democrats to gain their advice on prospective nominees to the Supreme Court before seeking consent.[34] In today's partisan climate, such bipartisanship is unheard of, but it happened only thirty-two years ago just as the constitution envisions. Justice Anthony Kennedy was chosen through that process, and became the moderate conservative swing vote on the high court for decades until his retirement in 2018. His confirmation wrapped up during the height of primary season to choose a successor to President Reagan.

BIDEN'S NEAR-DEATH EXPERIENCE

Justice Kennedy's nomination sailed through Congress on February 3, 1988, the with a one-hour floor debate and a 97–0 confirmation vote, but Senator Biden wasn't there to conduct the proceedings.[35] Instead, Joe Biden was in the hospital facing a dire health problem that required six months of convalescence after two surgeries to repair two brain aneurysms at Walter Reed Medical Center in Bethesda, Maryland.[36]

Biden began experiencing headaches during the holiday season soon after his forty-sixth birthday—leading him to carry around a bottle of Tylenol for the pain—culminating in a painful blackout in a Rochester,

New York, hotel room after a speech. He flew back to Wilmington the following morning and got checked out by a doctor, who determined that an artery on the right side of his brain had ruptured. Nine days after Justice Kennedy's confirmation, Biden went into a microsurgical craniotomy surgery.

Jill Biden acted as gatekeeper, ensuring her husband remained isolated during his recovery, which he described as the first time he was "really rested."

He told a crowd of hundreds that that he had received a "second chance in life" as he returned to public life at a Delaware Democratic Party event, according to the *Delaware News Journal*. "That last year had taught me one big lesson: The only things that are truly urgent are matters of life and death," Biden wrote in his *New York Times* best-selling memoir *Promises to Keep*.[37] "I was no less committed or passionate, but I no longer felt I had to win every moment to succeed. More important I understood that a single moment of failure—even one so public and wounding as the end of my presidential campaign—could not determine my epitaph."

It did not.

he last twenty years of Senator Biden's career in Congress, his "second chance," saw him take a greater role in foreign affairs and pass some consequential legislation, as well as holding more consequential judiciary committee hearings over the final seven years of his chairmanship. Those saw him go from pushing "get tough on crime" initiatives to starting to undo some of that work. The senator took two major votes on Iraq, the second as chairman of the Senate Committee on Foreign Relations.

Senator Biden held hearings about Iraq in the run-up to the Gulf War, which he opposed. As he took on more responsibility over foreign affairs in the Senate, Biden oversaw another set of controversial Supreme Court hearings over a nominee from a Republican president, but with different results that continue to spark debate to this day. Then, Biden had a major role in being the primary sponsor of a mammoth 1994 crime bill which passed the Senate with a 95–4 bipartisan majority and is becoming one of the most discussed topics of the 2020 Democratic primary.

As the ranking member of the Senate Committee on Foreign Relations in the late 1990s, and its chairman twice in the following decade, Joe Biden left a major impact on American foreign policy, though he also gathered critics in the process. As the senator from a state with a high concentration of financial companies, Biden sponsored a major bank-ruptcy reform bill, which his 2020 Democratic primary opponent Senator Elizabeth Warren (D-MA) spent years fighting. After the 9/11 terrorist attack, Biden played a key role in crafting the 2002 authorization of use of military force (AUMF) that President George W. Bush used to take America to war in Iraq. By then, he had become his party's leading voice on foreign affairs.

In fact, it would be Senator Biden's long experience in foreign policy matters that became one of the main reasons he concluded his career in Congress when his then-colleague Senator Barack Obama (D-IL) chose him to be his running mate in 2008, and they won the election.

After recovering from his major health scare, Senator Biden continued his chairmanship of the judiciary committee and, after fifteen years on the Foreign Affairs Committee in 1990, he began taking on duties in America's United Nations delegation for the first time. At the same time, President George H. W. Bush had a pair of Supreme Court openings to fill when two longtime liberal members of the court departed, leading to more hearings with Chairman Biden.

On July 22, 1990, senior Justice William Brennan—a progressive champion for decades—announced his retirement due to medical issues at the age of eighty-four, setting off speculation that Bush would move the court far to the right.[1] Three days later, President Bush chose to nominate David Souter, a little-known judge from New Hampshire, to take his place. He had been considered for the seat Justice Kennedy took in 1988, and his limited paper trail was considered a major strength in his nomination. Judge Souter's four-day nomination hearings took place in mid-September 1990, not unlike the Bork hearings, and with open grass-roots opposition from the National Association for the Advancement of Colored People (NAACP) and the National Organization for Women (NOW).[2] Despite sharp rhetoric and "no" votes from both of Massachusetts Democratic senators, Souter was confirmed 90–9 in a massively bipartisan vote, though conservatives would later be irate at his moderate bent on the court.

BIDEN VOTES AGAINST FIRST WAR IN IRAQ

Senator Biden argued forcefully against rushing to war in Iraq, which in retrospect appears wise, but finished in the minority of that vote and endured sharp criticism for his opposition.

In August 1990, Iraq invaded Kuwait, leading to a chain of events that has kept a major U.S. military presence in the Persian Gulf ever since. The small oil-producing nation had a maritime alliance with the U.S. dating to 1987, which sought to ensure that eleven of its oil tankers could move freely through the gulf.[3] President George H. W. Bush marshaled America's diplomatic strength and pushed the United Nations to approve action to liberate Kuwait from its invader, led by dictator Saddam Hussein.

At the end of 1990, Senator Biden chaired hearings on the problems in Iraq. "All evidence indicates that the world embargo against Iraq is the most comprehensive in history. Collectively, we've imposed nothing less than a state of siege on that outlaw regime," said Biden on the dais. "A policy, backed by this dispatch of a powerful deterrent force that was accepted by Congress and the American people as early as early August."[4]

He also expressed concern about the endgame of a war in Iraq, which proved to be prescient, since America's actions in the Gulf War—particularly Bush's call to instigate an internal rebellion—led to a slaughter of the majority Shiite Muslims by Hussein's Sunni supporters who held power.[5]

"What's the hurry for war? What's the hurry?" asked Delaware Democratic Senator Joe Biden in what the *Toronto Star* called a "grim" congressional debate.[6] He concluded his floor remarks in the debate about an authorization of use of military force in Iraq by saying: "Mr. President Bush, if you are listening, I implore you to understand that even if you win today, you still lose. The Senate and the Nation are divided on this issue, Mr. President. [T]he debate to punish Saddam Hussein, the impatience you feel, the anger you feel are all justified, but none of them add up to vital interests, and none of them—none of them justify the death of our sons and daughters. To quote a businessman who has been quoted before on this floor, Mr. President: 'First, commit this nation, then commit our troops. We will finish whatever you start.' Mr. President, the sons of this generation are patriotic, as are the daughters. We will finish it. But for God's sake, don't start it unless you think it is a vital interest, which I feel strongly it is not."[7]

Senator Biden voted against going to war, but the Senate approved its resolution authorizing President Bush to proceed 52–47 with ten Democrats crossing party lines and only two Republicans in opposition. The House voted 250–183 in favor of war in Iraq with only one in three Democrats supporting the action.[8] It was called the "100 Hours War." Gen. Colin Powell captured Kuwait quickly but, fearing the kind of disintegration that was to be seen after the Iraq War, America's military didn't depose Hussein. Yet it never left the region.[9]

However, at the same time Biden was in favor staying out of Iraq, it's important to note that he supported U.S. intervention to stop the genocide of Muslims in Bosnia after Yugoslavia collapsed in the wake of the end of Soviet communism.[10]

CONTROVERSIAL SUPREME COURT HEARINGS EXPOSE SEXUAL HARASSMENT IN THE AMERICAN WORKPLACE

In October 1991, Justice Thurgood Marshall, a legendary liberal jurist, retired from the Supreme Court. He had been the NAACP's general counsel before becoming the first African American to serve as US solicitor general and to sit on the Supreme Court. The Bush administration wasted little time in sending a controversially conservative nomination to replace Marshall: the DC circuit court's Judge Clarence Thomas, a far-right jurist who had been unanimously confirmed to that role only sixteen months earlier by a voice vote of the Senate.[11]

Four years after the Bork hearings, the Senate judiciary committee's hearings on Clarence Thomas's nomination to the Supreme Court— similarly held fourteen months before a general election—would generate just as much controversy, but an even longer-lasting impact on American politics. For starters, senate Democrats were outraged that the Republican president would nominate an African American jurist who opposed affirmative action and the civil rights movement to replace a legend of the civil rights era. Secondly, Thomas was a former Reagan political appointee with little experience on the bench, but one with a reliably far-right viewpoint in his lectures and speeches.

The Bush administration was warned by its attorney general that Judge Thomas's nomination would be divisive, then was embarrassed when he only won a "qualified" rating from the American Bar Association (ABA) and not the higher rating of "well qualified."[12] An African American activist, lawyer, and member of NOW, Florynce "Flo" Kennedy, memorably said about Thomas's Supreme Court nomination, "We'll Bork him."[13]

Senator Biden led the hearings, while once again Senator Kennedy led the opposition to Thomas's nomination. The Delaware senator challenged the jurist on legal grounds, extracting the meaning of his speeches about "natural law"—a philosophy without a written basis in the text of the law—during his questioning. The *New York Times* noted that if confirmed, Thomas would be the first justice in over fifty years to give credence to "natural law" theories. (By way of comparison in today's Supreme Court, recently confirmed Trump appointee Justice Neil Gorsuch subscribes to a "moral reading" view of jurisprudence under "natural law" concepts.[14])

But that wouldn't be the issue that generated so much controversy that Justice Thomas's liberal detractors are still debating if he should be impeached for his congressional confirmation testimony after viewing it through the lens of the modern "Me Too" movement.

President Reagan first appointed Thomas as the assistant secretary of the U.S. Department of Education's Office for Civil Rights in 1981, and he hired a young lawyer named Anita Hill as his assistant. Like Thomas, she had been trained at Yale. When Reagan later named Thomas as the head of the Equal Employment Opportunity Commission (EEOC) in 1982, Hill transferred positions to keep working with him, then quit in 1983 to become a professor of law at the private evangelical school Oral Roberts University in Tulsa, Oklahoma. She had commented negatively on Thomas's time at the EEOC to the *Washington Post* in early September when he criticized her sister for being on welfare.[15] "It takes a lot of detachment to publicize a person's experience in that way" and "a certain kind of self-centeredness not to recognize some of the programs that benefited you," Hill told the *Washington Post,* whose reporters were unaware that she had filed a sworn affidavit with the Senate judiciary committee recounting a story of workplace sexual harassment by Thomas. "I think he doesn't understand people, he doesn't relate to people who don't make it on their own."

In late September, NPR's Nina Totenberg noticed something amiss in the Senate judiciary committee's proceedings when Biden briefly mentioned questions about Thomas's character, but they still voted Thomas out of committee on October 1—however with no recommendation, itself an unusual choice.[16] That led her to investigate, and when Totenberg started asking around, she heard Hill's story and contacted her for an interview. The law professor declined unless the radio journalist had a copy of her affidavit, which a member of the committee leaked to her. The result set off a political firestorm in the Senate that rippled out across America's workplace culture in the twenty-eight years since.

"After a brief discussion of work, he would turn the conversation to a discussion of sexual matters. His conversations were very vivid," said Anita Hill about Clarence Thomas to NPR in that explosive interview. "He spoke about acts that he had seen in pornographic films involving such matters as women having sex with animals and films showing group sex or rape scenes." In fact, the committee had asked the White House to have the FBI investigate Hill's allegations and both she and Thomas were interviewed before his nomination was sent to the full Senate.[17]

Thomas's confirmation to the Supreme Court had seemed on track before the NPR interview and Hill's subsequent press conference, but the resulting hearings seared the issue of workplace sexual harassment into the national consciousness. Senator Biden's role was to run the hearings as a neutral arbiter, but critics believe that he overstepped those bounds with his subsequent questioning of Anita Hill during four days of supplemental hearings after her incendiary revelations, as well as being faulted for allowing Republicans on the committee to level vicious attacks against her.[18]

"He talked about pornographic materials depicting individuals with large penises or large breasts, involved in various sex acts. On several occasions, Thomas told me graphically of his own sexual prowess," she told Congress in sworn testimony. Her most sensational allegation was that Thomas told her he spotted a "pubic hair on my Coke." In turn, the judge attacked the proceedings as unfair to him, saying, "From my standpoint, as a black American, as far as I'm concerned, it is a high-tech lynching for uppity blacks who in any way deign to think for themselves, to do for themselves, to have different ideas."

Totenberg told NPR in a 2016 interview that she was publicly vilified by the Senate, along with Anita Hill, and that she was so afraid they'd turn everything into an official proceeding that she burned her notes. Senators later tried to compel her to testify in a leak hunt, but stopped short of a contempt proceeding, letting her source remain secret.

The biggest issue critics have with Senator Biden's handling of the Thomas hearings is that he didn't call witnesses who could've corroborated Hill's story, but did call four witnesses backing up the nominee. His actions then have become a present political problem that Joe Biden is already confronting on the campaign trail, and, in November 2018, he apologized publicly to Anita Hill for his poor handling of her questioning.[19] But she said his lack of an express apology during a one-on-one phone call in 2019 fell short of her expectations.[20] Justice Thomas won an up-or-down confirmation vote 52–48 on October 15, 1991; it would be the slimmest confirmation margin for a Supreme Court justice in American history until the nomination of Brett Kavanaugh in 2018.

The political fallout from that hearing inspired what has been dubbed as the "Year of The Woman" in 1992, resulting in four new female senators—including the first black woman and the first Jewish woman— where before there had only been two woman in the upper chamber of Congress.[21] Twenty-four women won new seats in the House, double the prior membership. Today there are twenty-five women serving in the Senate with a two-to-one margin of Democrats to Republicans. It also led to sweeping awareness of workplace sexual assault and a doubling of reported claims in just the year after the Thomas hearings, which revealed that women were being mistreated all over America. Congress also responded by expanding women's rights to be free of sexual harassment in the workplace—after the Supreme Court had curtailed them in rulings—when it passed the Civil Rights Act of 1991 and President Bush signed it into law, after having vetoed a more sweeping measure the year before.[22]

THE BIDEN CRIME BILL: PLUSES AND MINUSES

In his eighth and final year as Senate judiciary chairman, Joe Biden passed his largest piece of legislation: the sweeping Violent Crime Control and Law Enforcement Act of 1994, best known as the "Crime Bill." It was the new Democratic president's top priority, and Biden had wanted to pass comprehensive legislation to fight crime since becoming chair. Most Americans cited violent crime as their top concern in the late 1980s and through the 1990s. Also, in the wake of Democrats' loss in the 1988 presidential election loss, the party had struggled to deflect a "soft on crime" image.[23]

President Clinton signed the crime bill into law on September 13, 1994, and up until the last few years had considered it his signature accomplishment by allocating funds to hire 100,000 new police officers.[24] Senator Biden also touted his role in passing the bill, which allocated the billions needed toward prison construction to fuel the now-discredited get-tough policy known as "mass incarceration."

However, the crime bill wasn't a total failure; it included a federal assault weapons ban and the Violence Against Women Act (VAWA), as well as mandating public registries for sexual offenders by September 1997, and included provisions to protect the information that citizens give to states to obtain driver's licenses, which had been used to harass abortion providers. In actuality, Senator Biden has called the enactment of VAWA his "proudest" legislative achievement.

But it also legalized the federal death penalty again (it has been used three times since then, and sixty-three people are on the federal death row) and eliminated Pell grants for prisoners to obtain higher education. Still, the crime bill's expanded sentencing, a "three strikes" law, and new criminal statutes amping up drug-related penalties all interacted with Biden's prior legislation to enhance the federal government's Drug War to send hundreds of thousands of Americans to prison and create a trend at the state level to lock up more—often nonviolent—offenders. The senator personally opposed "three strikes" and warned that states would mimic the legislation if it passed, but kept the language as part of a grand compromise.[25]

Incarceration skyrocketed even as crime fell; America now has over 22 percent of the world's prisoners but only 4.4 percent of its population.[26] In particular, the tougher sentencing for crack cocaine versus powder cocaine would contribute heavily to harsher sentences in the African American community, even though the two substances are the same. By 2015, many states had more citizens in prisons than living on college campuses.[27]

The Department of Justice published a summary of its many provisions. The crime bill added funds for gun background checks, ended sales to domestic abusers, and established higher federal licensure standards for gun dealers.[28] It created new categories of insurance and telemarketing frauds, and gave new rights to crime victims as well as restitution rights to the victims of sex offenders and child molesters. Lastly, it defined new categories of crime and enhanced penalties for drive-by shootings, using semiautomatic weapons in a crime, and gun trafficking, as well as hate crimes. Unfortunately, the bill's allocation of nearly a billion dollars for "Byrne grants" drove thousands of local police departments to ramp up their drug task forces, which fueled mass incarceration because the federal aid applications prioritized arrest numbers.[29] Many of those arrests happened in communities of color.

As a result, in 2007, Senator Biden introduced the Drug Sentencing Reform and Cocaine Kingpin Trafficking Act of 2007, which sought to eliminate the crack versus cocaine sentencing disparity that had originally been codified by his 1994 legislation and repealing the mandatory minimum sentences for possession of small amounts.[30] Congress took three more years to pass a similar reform called the Fair Sentencing Act of 2010, but that act wouldn't be applied retroactively until the First Step Act surprisingly passed in the waning days of 2018.[31] Five years after President Obama signed the Fair Sentencing Act, half as many people were prosecuted for crack possession than before the act was signed, and sentencing was similar to that for possession of the powdered form of the drug.[32] Biden also supported the Second Chance Act, which became law in April 2008 and funded a dozen different programs aimed at ending mass incarceration and assisting in inmate reentry for the purpose of reducing recidivism.[33]

The federal assault weapon ban in Senator Biden's crime bill was one of its signature initiatives and a law whose benefits aged well until Congress let it expire in 2004. It came about because of two particularly egregious mass shootings in California and Texas, and after the infamous "101 California Street" shooting in San Francisco. It banned the manufacture and sale of new semiautomatic rifles and high-capacity magazines for ten years, but Congress let it sunset after it became a polarizing issue in American politics alongside the rise of the National Rifle Association (NRA) as a political force. The NRA's influence crested in 2016 when it spent a record $30 million on President Trump's election, but is crumbling as of early June 2019 in the midst of revelations of its ties to Russia and insider self-enrichment. Passing the assault weapons ban was a courageous act by Biden and will surely yield plaudits in the 2020 Democratic primary, which is taking place among an epidemic of mass shootings and gun violence in America.

Senator Biden's role in passing the Violence Against Women Act (VAWA) cannot be understated. He introduced the act in 1990 and on its twentieth anniversary in 1994 explained why he prioritized its passage as Senate judiciary chairman in a *Time* magazine article:

> Twenty years ago, this was a right that few people understood and our culture failed to recognize. Kicking a wife in the stomach or pushing her down the stairs was repugnant, but it wasn't taken seriously as a crime. It was considered a "family affair." State authorities assumed if a woman was beaten or raped by her husband or someone she knew, she must have deserved it. It was a "lesser crime" to rape a woman if she was a "voluntary companion." Many state murder laws still held on to the notion that if your wife left you and you killed her, she had provoked it and you had committed manslaughter.
>
> That was the tragic history when, as chairman of the Senate Judiciary Committee, I introduced the Violence Against Women Act in 1990. We started out believing that the only way to change the culture was to expose the toll of domestic violence on American families. And I was convinced, as I am today, that the basic decency of the

American people would demand change once they saw the scale of violence and the depth of the ignorance and stereotypes used to justify it.

As a consequence of the law, domestic violence rates have dropped 64 percent; billions of dollars have been averted in social and medical costs; and we've had higher rates of convictions for special-victims units and fundamental reforms of state laws. The nation's first National Domestic Violence Hotline has helped 3.4 million women and men fight back from domestic and dating violence. And along the way we've changed the culture. Abuse is violent and ugly and today there is rightful public outrage over it. It matters that the American people have sent a clear message: you're a coward for raising a hand to a woman or child—and you're complicit if you fail to condemn it.

VAWA is a law that requires reauthorization every five years, upon which it has often been expanded since 1994. For the first time since Biden helped pass VAWA, the lame-duck Republican-controlled Congress allowed it to expire at the end of 2018.[34] While its funding is secure, the act is still awaiting reauthorization as of June 2019, even though the Democratic-controlled House voted overwhelmingly to reauthorize the law in April 2019.[35] The bill has hit a roadblock in the Senate, where its "red flags" provision—which allows for victims of domestic violence to obtain a court order for the confiscation of the offenders' weapons—has drawn criticism from some Republicans and conservative lobbying groups like the NRA.[36]

In 2003, the last crime bill Biden sponsored passed into law. The Illicit Drug Anti-Proliferation Act targeted property owners who hosted night-clubs and parties known as raves, where people used drugs.[37] The ACLU disparaged Biden's bill as giving the Drug Enforcement Administration too much power to chill free speech and shut down electronic music events.[38]

THE BANKRUPTCY BILL

Senator Biden's home state of Delaware is the jurisdiction of choice for corporate domiciles in the United States because of its tax advantages, privacy of ownership, and a court of chancery that leaves decisions to judges, not juries.[39] It's also the home of many credit card companies, including then third-largest card issuer MBNA, which spent years pushing for a bill that would make it more difficult for consumers to discharge their debts through bankruptcy. Biden's son Hunter worked at MBNA, and the corporation were a major contributor to the senator's campaigns.[40]

"I'm not the senator from MBNA," said Biden to the *Washington Post* in 1999 after he had shot down an extremely creditor-friendly bankruptcy bill the year before. But in a rebuke of the Democratic Party's older economic policies, Biden said, "I'm not the senator from 1979, either."[41] Senator Biden introduced the Bankruptcy Reform Act. His longtime friend in the senate, Ted Kennedy, denounced the bill, while Kennedy's son Patrick endorsed the bill as the U.S. Representative from Rhode Island. His bill passed Congress, but because of then-Professor Warren's efforts to sway First Lady Hillary Clinton, the president vetoed the bill in late 2000 before leaving office. *Politico* reports that the Delaware senator was genuinely concerned about bankruptcy abuses and said so during a hearing on a new bankruptcy reform bill:

> *"Creditors are not people I am crazy about," Biden said during a hearing in 2001, noting that he had refinanced his home in order to send his children to college. "But I start off with the proposition that something is rotten in Denmark, as the old expression used to be," he added. "An awful lot of people are discharging debt who shouldn't. This voluminous increasing in filing—it is exponential what has happened. Something is up, and that happened when the economy was booming, absolutely booming." The rising bankruptcy rate was driving up prices for everybody else, he argued, including "people where I come from. So I am so sick of this self-righteous sheen put on anybody who wants to tighten up bankruptcy is really anti-debtor," Biden said. "People are getting hurt."*[42]

"Senator Biden supports legislation that will fall hardest on women, particularly on women trying to rear children on their own," wrote Professor Warren in the *Harvard Women's Law Journal.* Her specialty is bankruptcy law, and the Harvard professor advocated tirelessly against bankruptcy reformers who were not using the extensive data she collaged and wrote about in her bestselling book, *The Two-Income Trap.* Families were declaring bankruptcy at an ever-increasing rate due to medical bills, job loss or a combination of all of the above. But the bills focused on the few people who ran up large debts and abused the bankruptcy system to shirk those debts, a popular anecdote that wasn't rooted in fact.

After President George W. Bush's election, the bankruptcy bill was resurrected in 2001, though it failed to pass Congress. But it had Senator Biden's vote (and New York Senator Hillary Clinton's vote as well, shocking Warren). Three months before the bill passed, Professor Warren and Biden faced off in a Senate judiciary committee meeting on opposite sides of the bill. He called her arguments against the bill, which were the result of extensive study, "compelling" and "mildly demagogic" and asked her whom to blame for excessive consumer debt. Warren blamed lenders for excessive fees and interest, and many confusing financial products that took advantage of consumers. Biden tried to deflect, saying that Warren's arguments pertained more to usury, the practice of making unethically expensive loans. *Politico* reported the exchange:

> "Maybe we should talk about usury rates, then," he replied. "Maybe that is what we should be talking about, not bankruptcy." "Senator, I will be the first. Invite me." "I know you will, but let's call a spade a spade," Biden said. "Your problem with credit card companies is usury rates from your position. It is not about the bankruptcy bill." "But, senator," Warren countered, "if you are not going to fix that problem, you can't take away the last shred of protection from these families."

At this last remark, Biden smiled and sat back in his chair, according to Mallory Duncan, a lobbyist who was in the room. "I got it, OK," Biden said. "You are very good, professor." "It was like watching a championship tennis match," Duncan told me, more than a decade later, of the sparring between the two future presidential candidates.

In April 2005, both chambers of Congress passed the Bankruptcy Abuse and Consumer Protection Act in bipartisan fashion, with Biden's help, getting seventy-five votes in the Senate. Then-Senator Obama voted against it. President Bush signed it into law.

At the time, Senator Biden bragged that it would improve "the situation of women and children who depend on child support," because it required divorced parents to make child support payments ahead of all other payments except remittances to the bankruptcy trustee. The bill added a means test for people looking for a clean start through Chapter 7 bankruptcy, forcing many into Chapter 13 repayment programs that last up to five years. It has sharply curtailed filings by lower income people who can't afford legal counsel to navigate the thicket of paperwork required by the bill's means test. Since then, Biden has defended his role in the bill as working to moderate a bill that Republicans were bound to pass. "He was representing the interests of his state, which is one of the responsibilities of anybody elected to Congress," retired University of Delaware political scientist Joseph Pika told the *Delaware News Journal*, commenting on the bill.[43] He noted that, "progressives within the party are not going to be very happy about the position."

2002 AUTHORIZATION FOR USE OF MILITARY FORCE ON IRAQ

The hotly contested 2000 general election ended with President Bush beating Vice President Al Gore by barely over 500 votes in Florida. But it also left the Senate deadlocked at 50–50 with the vice president casting the tie-breaking vote, and unusually, determining control of the chamber with that vote in early 2001. For that reason, Joe Biden became chairman of the Senate Committee on Foreign Relations for seventeen days at the start of 2001, then the ranking member for three months. Then, when Vermont Republican Senator Jim Jeffords dropped his party affiliation and became an independent caucusing with Democrats, Biden once again became its chairman, which lasted for the remainder of the 107th Congress until January 2003.

It was a consequential moment in American foreign affairs, because the 9/11 attacks happened just six months into Biden's second term as chair. A group of nineteen Al Qaeda terrorists hijacked four planes and flew them into the World Trade Center and the Pentagon; a fourth flight crashed into a field in Pennsylvania after being hijacked.

A month later, Senator Biden emerged as the Democratic party's chief spokesman on foreign policy issues. He advocated for passage of the controversial Patriot Act, which expanded domestic surveillance with the goal of preventing future terrorist attacks. A *New Republic* article documented how Biden frequently reminded anyone who would listen that he had crafted a similar bill after the tragic Oklahoma City federal building bombing by a right-wing domestic terrorist, but didn't pass.[44] The rest of the article documented the Delaware senator's public speaking habits, including multiple gaffes the author believed he needed to tone down to be an effective leader whose advantages included his pro-NATO internationalist positions and his toughness. His relationships overseas after twenty-six years on the Foreign Affairs Committee were another strength. Biden's great weakness was a lack of brevity and the tendency to talk his way through problems in a stream-of-consciousness manner. In 2008, the *New York Times* summarized his position on Iraq:

> While Mr. Biden never linked Saddam Hussein's Iraq to Qaeda terrorists, he was concerned that the effort to maintain economic sanctions was faltering. While Iraq was not an imminent threat, its presumed programs to develop weapons of mass destruction, he argued, could become one, unless United Nations resolution on weapons inspections were strictly enforced. If military action was needed, he argued, it should be a last resort taken in concert with other nations. The dismantlement of Iraq's weapons programs, not the toppling of Mr. Hussein, he said, should be the goal.[45]

As chairman, Biden played a key role in supporting the formal Authorization for Use of Military Force (AUMF) that enabled President Bush to send American troops to war in Iraq, and he voted in favor of the resolution. He stated bluntly that, "One thing is clear: These weapons must be dislodged from Saddam, or Saddam must be dislodged from power. If we wait for the danger from Saddam to become clear, it could be too late."[46] In a reversal from his position on the Gulf War, Biden told the Senate that he didn't believe President George W. Bush was in a rush to war, which he accused his father of perpetrating in 1991.[47]

His opponent Senator Bernie Sanders is the only other candidate who was in Congress at the time, and he used his vote in the House of Representatives against the war, offering five specific reasons why he was opposed the invasion.[48] "Sadly, much of what I feared," Sanders tweeted in early 2019, "in fact did happen."

Bush's Iraq War AUMF passed Congress with seventy-seven votes in the Senate—only one Republican voted against it—and 296 votes in the House, including eighty-one Democratic votes for and six Republicans dissenting.[49] It was a tremendous strategic blunder by America's government, primarily because the White House lied about key evidence to convince the public that Iraqi dictator Saddam Hussein was on the verge of acquiring nuclear weapons and politically linked him with Al Qaeda terrorists, but those ties didn't exist. Even widely respected General Colin Powell, who gave the key speech in support of the war as Bush's first secretary of state, called it a "blot" on his record and a "great intelligence failure."[50] Later, it was revealed that President Bush put his top political adviser in charge of the "White House Iraq Group," an arm of his administration whose sole purpose was to misrepresent top-secret intelligence to drive the country into war.[51]

★★★

The broad language of the 2002 AUMF continues to authorize U.S. troop deployments to this day, because it specified that the president could deploy forces to deal with problems arising from Iraq without geographical limitation, not the country's government at the time.[52] Since the AUMF, two Democratic nominees who voted for the war, John Kerry and Hillary Clinton, both lost general elections for president; Barack Obama, who publicly opposed the Iraq war, won handily.

As the Iraq war dragged on, Senator Biden continued to present policy ideas to salvage the situation after the Bush administration sparked an endless insurgency war by ordering the dissolution of the Iraqi Army and a policy of punishing Saddam Hussein's former political party members called "de-Baathification."[53] The Biden-Gelb plan was outlined in a *Times* op-ed the senator coauthored with Leslie H. Gelb, the head of the Council on Foreign Relations. They argued that Iraq needed a federated government that gave local autonomy to the three main ethnic groups in the country, who shared a government because of British colonial machinations, not Iraqi nationalism. The two men wrote:

> *Now the Bush administration, despite its profound strategic misjudgments in Iraq, has a similar opportunity. To seize it, however, America must get beyond the present false choice between "staying the course" and "bringing the troops home now" and choose a third way that would wind down our military presence responsibly while preventing chaos and preserving our key security goals.*

> *The idea, as in Bosnia, is to maintain a united Iraq by decentralizing it, giving each ethno-religious group—Kurd, Sunni Arab and Shiite Arab—room to run its own affairs, while leaving the central government in charge of common interests. We could drive this in place with irresistible sweeteners for the Sunnis to join in, a plan designed by the military for withdrawing and redeploying American forces, and a regional nonaggression pact.*

Critics immediately labeled the plan a "soft partition," and the Senate passed a resolution 73–25 in favor of Biden's idea.[54] Eight years later, after former Bush and Obama Defense Secretary Robert Gates savaged Biden's foreign policy judgement in his memoir, *Politico*'s Josh Gerstein examined the Biden-Gelb plan and wrote that, "While Biden may have taken a beating repeatedly in recent years for some foreign policy calls he's made, his judgment on Iraq's capacity to stay united now looks almost prescient."[55]

BIDEN'S SECOND PRESIDENTIAL CAMPAIGN

Senator Joe Biden embarked on his second campaign for the presidency of the United States on January 31, 2007, during an appearance with NBC's Tim Russert on *Meet the Press,* telling him cheekily that he planned to be himself and the "best Biden he can be."[56] He joked to ABC's Diane Sawyer on *Good Morning America* that he was the "800th candidate" to declare a campaign for the open seat; he was the seventh Democrat in the race and eight Republicans were already in the primary.[57] Biden entered the race as the sitting chairman of the Senate Committee on Foreign Relations.

Unfortunately, the senator's best behavior didn't even last through the day, and his controversial remarks about his top opponents, Senator Hillary Clinton and Senator Obama, backfired spectacularly. In an interview with the *New York Observer* newspaper and the GMA interview, Biden brutally savaged Clinton's foreign policy ideas. It was the kind of strong statement that played well in congressional battles, but not in a fight within the party. But it was his remarks about Obama that mortally wounded his campaign before it ever really got off the ground.

He told the *Observer* that the junior Illinois senator was, "the first mainstream African American [presidential candidate] who is articulate and bright and clean and a nice-looking guy. I mean, that's a storybook, man."[58] In an afternoon conference call he showered Obama with praise as "a superstar" according to the *Washington Post*, who caught "lightning in a jar." Biden called to apologize to Barack Obama, who released a statement saying he "didn't take Senator Biden's comments personally," but only partly "absolved" his opponent. Obama pointed out that Biden was historically inaccurate, noting that, "African American presidential candidates like Jesse Jackson, Shirley Chisholm, Carol Moseley Braun, and Al Sharpton gave a voice to many important issues through their campaigns, and no one would call them inarticulate."

The *Washington Post* reported that Biden released a written statement later that day in which he continued to walk back what he had said: "I deeply regret any offense my remark in the *New York Observer* might have caused anyone. That was not my intent and I expressed that to Senator

Obama." But the damage was done. Senator Biden had trouble attracting donors and crowds after that gaffe, even though other candidates adopted so much of his foreign policy platform, that his campaign produced an ad called "Joe's right" showing the other primary candidates agreeing with him on the debate stage.[59] Pundits called Biden's debate performances "surprisingly disciplined," but he just never gained traction with voters.[60] His most memorable quote from the campaign trail was a takedown of Rudy Giuliani, who was at the time a candidate in the Republican primary. Biden said of Giuliani that there are "only three things he [needs] to make . . . a sentence: a noun and a verb and 9/11."[61] Drake University political science professor Dennis Goldford told the *Post* that he was having rhetorical trouble switching target audiences from elected officials to regular voters.[62] "He talks like a senator, not a president. The forest gets lost in the trees."

Joe Biden won only 4 percent of votes in the Iowa caucus, good for just 0.9 percent of the delegates and fifth place. Unlike his first presidential campaign, there was no drama or media firestorm involved in Biden's decision to leave the race. He dropped out of the race the following day, as did Connecticut Senator Chris Dodd, who finished seventh in the six-person field, behind delegates uncommitted to any candidate.[63] What happened eight months later was a feel-good conclusion to Senator Biden's thirty-six-year career in Congress and transformed his political career: Barack Obama chose him to be his running mate in the 2008 presidential election.

ANALYSIS OF JOE BIDEN'S CHANCES FOR WINNING THE NOMINATION AND PRESIDENCY

J oe Biden announced his 2020 Democratic primary bid on April 25, 2019 by releasing a powerful three-minute video about the "battle for the soul of this nation." Leading up to the announcement, he sat atop the national polls, topping all states but Iowa by a wide margin. Biden would go on to officially launch his campaign with a six-thousand-person rally on a sunny May afternoon in the heavily Democratic city of Philadelphia.[1] He spoke about unity. Since then and leading up to the first Democratic debates, he has remained in the front-runner's position above a Democratic primary field that has ballooned to twenty-three contestants as of June 2019.[2] The former vice president fretted about raising enough cash before declaring his run, but hauled in $6.3 million in just his first day.[3] Biden called one of his campaign donors the following day—a grad student named Josh—to personally thank him, and posted his side of the conversation to Twitter.[4]

Biden is betting his campaign on his favorable public image as President Obama's vice president, his long experience in international affairs, and his guy-next-door personality. He stands to benefit the most from the Democratic primary's proportional representation system, which only gives delegates to candidates who win more than 15 percent of the vote, because, among all candidates, he's the only one who stands above that number across most polls in most states in the early going of the campaign.

Joe Biden's ideology is one of personal connection and moderate policy. He has not released a detailed domestic agenda as of early June 2019, but his foreign policy experience makes him a reliable liberal internationalist and supporter of the NATO alliance.

"I think Joe Biden is clearly someone who is in the center left, but he is not perceived as an ideologue, in part because his career has spanned a length of time in which the Democratic Party has, frankly, moved a bit. So you can go back in his record and see things that today are considered rather conservative, looking at the 1994 crime bill," says *Washington Post* reporter and opinion columnist Jennifer Rubin, who is also an MSNBC contributor. "His views, I think it's fair to say, have changed. I don't say that as a negative thing. I say that as, frankly, a statement of admiration, that when events change, when problems are different, he has, in fact, changed. I think there's something a bit refreshing about that. I tend towards the practical and the pragmatic myself, so I kind of like that."[5]

Biden's personal memoir, *Promise Me, Dad*, is a best seller and takes readers inside what was his greatest challenge: maintaining his highly visible role as vice president while caring for and later grieving for his cancer-stricken, beloved eldest son, Beau. Joe Biden is heavily focused on high-impact emotional messaging in the early campaign, not policy specifics, aside from expanding Obamacare by adding a "public option." Recent polling from the nonprofit Kaiser Family Foundation finds that public support is very high to treat health care as a right, which Biden is supporting, but he's in favor of expanding the Affordable Care Act, and opposed to Senator Bernie Sanders's platform under the banner of Medicare for All.[6] He does not support the Green New Deal proposed by Rep. Alexandria Ocasio-Cortez (D-NY), but released a climate change proposal in early June 2019 that does call for its major feature: a national crash program to reach net zero carbon dioxide emissions by 2050 and an investment of $1.7 trillion over ten years into clean energy and other initiatives, according to the *New York Times*. As a senator, Joe Biden filed his first climate change bill in 1987, but he is the only candidate out of the top five in the polls as of early June 2019, who doesn't support Ocasio-Cortez's concept of a crash plan to fight climate change.[7]

"I don't think you can underestimate the degree to which the American people feel very affectionately towards Joe Biden," says Rubin, who became a conservative opinion columnist writing the "Right Turn Blog" for the *Washington Post* in 2011, after leaving behind her career as a Los Angeles labor lawyer and moving to Virginia. "He has become a fixture in politics, and he earned great respect from Democrats, because he was at the side of Barack Obama for eight years, and from non-Democrats in the way he has handled personal tragedy throughout his life. There is a sense . . . Perhaps a false sense, because we do not know politicians on an intimate basis, but there is a perception among many Americans that they know him. They like him. He's comfortable. He is someone who they may not agree with, who certainly has his faults, but is basically a good, decent guy. That does count for a lot in politics. He really is seen as an antidote to Trump, both in the fact that he may be perceived, rightly or wrongly, as someone who would be competitive with Trump and would beat Trump."

"America is unique in all of the world. America, folks, is an idea, an idea stronger than any army, bigger than any ocean. More powerful than any dictator or tyrant," said Biden at his kickoff rally just thirty miles north of his longtime hometown of Wilmington, Delaware.[8] "It offers hope to the tired, the poor, your huddled masses, to breathe free. It is written on the Statue of Liberty. We seem to have given up on that. America guarantees everyone, and I mean everyone, be treated with dignity. America gives hate no safe harbor." He continued:

> *Folks, that's what we believe. That's who we are. And I believe America has always been at its best when America has acted as one America, one America. One America may be a simple notion, but it doesn't make it any less profound. This nation needs to come together. It has to come together. Folks, we started this campaign when we did. I said I was running for three reasons. The first is to restore the soul of the nation, the essence of who we are. I mean it. And the second is to rebuild the backbone of this nation. And the third, to unite this nation, one America. One America.*
>
> *Folks, I know some of the really smart folks say Democrats don't want to hear about unity. They say*

Democrats are so angry, that the angrier a candidate can be, the better chance he or she has to win the Democratic nomination. Well, I don't believe it. I really don't. . . . I believe Democrats want to unify this nation. That's what our party has always been about.

The Biden campaign's historic parallel that may be the "closest to George Bush, 41," says Rubin, who left the Republican party in May 2016 after a Donald Trump presidential nomination was assured with a "Dear GOP" letter.[9] "He was at the side of a popular president, and he was seen as a good and decent man. He was seen as expert in operating the machinery of government, that he was a devoted family man. So I think he would be a very good parallel, actually."

"I absolutely think it could come down to a Biden/Warren face-off. I've been predicting for a couple weeks yet that she's going to pass Bernie Sanders, who seems kind of like old news to many Democrats, because he's running virtually the identical campaign that he did in 2016," says Rubin, who noted that Sanders voted in favor of Biden's now-controversial 1994 crime bill, which is sure to become a campaign issue with Biden, its primary sponsor, in the race. "She has been able to make the most of her voracious appetite for policy and her incredible energy in developing and churning out and advocating these policies, which are all in service of a single theme that is the system is rigged. She has done that better than anybody else." In a column in the *Washington Post* in late May 2019 she wrote an analysis of Biden's solid chances of winning the Democratic nomination entitled, "When the field thins, Joe Biden still may be on top":

Democratic insiders often seem to be on the lookout for former vice president Joe Biden's imminent demise. Well, no gaffes yet, but just you wait! That green energy plan—which he hasn't released—won't be progressive enough, you can bet on it! The presumption that it is only a matter of time before Biden collapses may rest on nothing more than wishful thinking. The data suggest he has a broad base of support.

[E]ven if one or more of this group falters, there is no guarantee someone else can consolidate the not-Biden vote. The Republican Echelon Poll, for example, found that in one-on-one match ups, Biden wins going away against Sanders (61/25), Harris (63/20), Buttigieg (65/17) and Warren (66/19). This is a single poll, a Republican one at that, but at this stage no single candidate seems capable of matching Biden's appeal.[10]

Biden's opponents are further handicapped by President Trump's predilection for attacking Biden, playing into Biden's "we're already in the general election" mode. In Trump's latest outrageous barb he aligned himself with North Korea's brutal dictator Kim Jong Un to slam Biden[.] In sum, Biden is hardly invincible. The debates provide opponents with the chance to level the playing field and Biden with a chance to slip up. However, Biden's stature gap, Trump's obsessive focus on him, and the evenly divided—but limited—support of his top rivals give him a solid chance of winning the nomination.[11]

"I don't think the major argument about Donald Trump in 2020 is going to be his personal offenses against women. I think it's going to be his policy offenses against women, his agenda and how, as we see now in the abortion bills rippling through the South and the Midwest, he has made the lives of women worse. Now, we are having this conversation before we've had a single debate, and the debates may very well change things." She continued:

He has, I think, in his corner, as well, one of the best assets one could possibly have, and that's Dr. Biden. People underestimate, or they have underestimated in the past, the benefit of a dynamic, popular, professional woman in providing that sort of credentials, that sort of stamp of approval to a male politician. I suspect he knows that. I think she's going to be used very generously. I think, as an experienced Second Lady, she's going to be a tremendous asset to him.

He certainly, I think, failed to pick up on subtle or not-so-subtle signals, but it was not sexual harassment or sexual assault in the same sense that Al Franken, that Donald Trump, others far more serious have been engaged in. I do think that criticism, going up to the campaign, in a way, was actually helpful to him. It was as if that issue got aired and dispensed with relatively quickly. According to polls, at least, Democratic voters really didn't care or they understood him well enough to say, "We've known this about Joe Biden for thirty years. We've been watching this guy. He's the huggy grandparent. He's the overly effusive uncle." So by and large, Democrats seem not to be very concerned about it.

At the end of May 2019, Biden is placing first in all of the seven major national polls, leading with an average of 34 percent according to *Real Clear Politics* He has led outright in all but two of *Real Clear Politics'* first fifty-four polls surveying the 2020 Democratic primary.[12]

Two weeks after launching his campaign, Biden ran solidly in first place in a Monmouth poll of the early primary state of New Hampshire with double the support of his second-ranked challenger, Sanders, whose home state is next door.[13] A Suffolk University poll in New Hampshire at the very end of April 2019 showed Biden ahead of the Vermont senator by eight points.[14]

Biden has a slim lead in the *Real Clear Politics* polling average for Iowa, which only considers high quality polls, the last of which happened in April 2019.[15] Three "C" rated polls on the data-driven politics website FiveThirtyEight.com have a wide range of results, with two of them showing Senator Sanders tied with Joe Biden; another shows Biden ahead by twenty-one points.[16]

Early Wisconsin polling in March 2019 showed Senator Sanders was the clear leader and Biden placed second with 24 percent of the vote, but that primary contest is relatively late in the 2020 primary season and a lot has happened since that poll.[17] A poll conducted in Florida by Bendixen & Amandi showed that Joe Biden is in first place with 26 percent of the vote, but 46 percent remain undecided one year out from the primary.

Biden polled in first in South Carolina with 45 percent of the projected vote in an early May 2019 poll by the *Charleston Post and Courier,* triple that of Sanders, his nearest opponent.[18]

Conventional wisdom is that Joe Biden will have to make a tremendous showing in South Carolina in 2020 if he wants to lay an early claim to the Democratic nomination, as well as winning a significant share of Iowa and New Hampshire's early primary delegates in order to winnow the field by Super Tuesday, which begins a heavy schedule of primaries set for March 2020.

"I think if he were to win South Carolina," says Rubin, who both covering the 2020 race and writing general assignment reporting about breaking news, "he might just [wrap] up the nomination much earlier than people anticipated. I think South Carolina is going to be extremely important. I think people are a bit surprised that the African American candidates in the race, so far, have not done as well as he has. I would remind people of Iowa and how that figured in the 2008 race. At the time, Barack Obama wasn't doing all that well with African Americans, either. He then won Iowa, and slowly, he gained the overwhelming support of the African American community. I think African Americans, perhaps more than any other group, appreciate just how vital it is to get rid of Donald Trump."

Biden's list of endorsements by late-May consists of five sitting U.S. senators and two former senators, as well as nine sitting U.S. Representatives and four former members of the House.[19] The current governors of

Delaware and New York have endorsed the former vice president, as well as several dozen state lawmakers. Celebrity endorsers include legendary filmmaker and frequent political pundit Rob Reiner, as well as *Game of Thrones* author George R. R. Martin.[20, 21]

The first votes in the 2020 Democratic primary race will be cast in New Hampshire in the days leading up to February 11, 2020. Primary campaigns are dynamic by their nature, and most often the early front-runner does not capture the party's nomination.

A RealClearPolitics average of the polling for a head-to-head matchup between Donald Trump and Biden shows the former vice president winning all seven tracked polls by at least five points; Rasmussen typically favors the president and it's the closest head to head poll between he and Biden. A Fox News poll in mid-May 2019 indicated an eleven-point gulf between the incumbent and his top challenger.[22] A Quinnipiac poll in Pennsylvania two weeks after Joe Biden's campaign launch showed him winning the theoretical matchup with Trump by a nine-point margin.[23]

Biden has an objectively easy-to-understand early path to becoming the Democratic nominee in 2020, but he has to convince the more liberal wing of the party that he'll fight for their policies, many of whom will likely try to push him on details of his past. However, it is always difficult for the early front-runner to maintain their lead through the primary and win, but if he only wins a plurality of pledged delegates, not a majority going in to the Democratic National Convention, which would lead to a "brokered convention," then he's got an excellent chance for superdelegates to give him the nod.[24] He's unlikely to be in the mix to be another candidate's running mate if he doesn't succeed in the primary, given his stature and the reasons why he wouldn't finish first. However, Joe Biden has the federal executive political experience that nobody else in the field holds, which gives him a leg up on the nomination.

"He's, in some ways, everything Trump is not. He's decent. He's kind. He's empathetic. He's experienced. He has a sense of the world. He understands the plight of the poor. He has been at the forefront of gay rights and gay marriage fights," concluded Rubin about the reasons Biden is leading all of the early polls. "If in every election, we choose the exact opposite of the president, Joe Biden is a pretty good candidate for that."

Joe Biden can definitely win the Democratic nomination, but he'll need to drive his message home to primary voters without getting tripped up by his past or the Republican attack machine, which is seeking to stop him by gearing up with a "goldmine of content" early in the primary.[25]

In some ways, he's like former President Lyndon B. Johnson, a career congressman from Texas who ascended to the vice presidency at the side of a storied younger leader. Johnson won reelection to the presidency against a Republican candidate whom he painted as an extremist in powerfully emotional advertising. Biden, who helped pass the Affordable Care Act, will have to convince his party's liberal base that he—like Johnson, who passed the Civil Rights Act in 1964 and the Great Society plan including Medicare—can also deploy his decades of experience to get bipartisan policy victories passed into law. His focus on electability makes Biden a formidable favorite to win the 2020 Democratic primary elections during a time when polls show 60 percent of Americans want a new president.[26]

NOTES

INTRODUCTION TO JOE BIDEN

1. Kruse, Michael. "How Grief Became Joe Biden's 'Superpower.'" *Politico.* Last modified January 25, 2019. https://www.politico.com/magazine /story/2019/01/25/joe-biden-2019-profile-grief-beau-car-accident-224178.

2. "Obama calls Biden 'the best vice president America has ever had.'" *Washington Post.* January 12, 2017. www.washingtonpost.com/video/politics /obama-calls-biden-the-best-vice-president-america-has-ever-had/2017/01 /12/69d915c8-d909-11e6-a0e6-d502d6751bc8_video.html.

3. McCaskill, Nolan D. "'They Don't Make 'em Like Joe Anymore': Biden Expands Grip on Congressional Endorsements." *Politico.* Last modified May 30, 2019. https://www.politico.com/story/2019/05/30/joe-biden -congressional-endorsements-1347598.

4. Raymond, Adam. "A Brief Guide to the Joe Biden, Anita Hill Controversy." *Intelligencer.* Last modified May 7, 2019. http://nymag.com/intelligencer /2019/05/guide-joe-biden-anita-hill-controversy.html.

5. Fandos, Nicholas. "Joe Biden's Role in '90s Crime Law Could Haunt Any Presidential Bid." *New York Times.* Last modified January 19, 2018. https:// www.nytimes.com/2015/08/22/us/politics/joe-bidens-role-in-90s-crime-law -could-haunt-any-presidential-bid.html.

6. Gadsden, Brett. "Here's How Deep Biden's Busing Problem Runs." *Politico.* Last modified May 5, 2019. https://www.politico.com/magazine/story/2019 /05/05/joe-biden-busing-problem-226791.

7. Itkowit, Colby. "'I get it': Joe Biden, accused of inappropriate physical con- tact by multiple women, says he will change his behavior." *Washington Post.* Last modified April 3, 2019. https://www.washingtonpost.com/politics/joe -biden-accused-of-inappropriate-physical-contact-by-multiple-women-says -he-will-change-his-behavior/2019/04/03/05b5ea58-5643-11e9-814f -e2f46684196e_story.html.

DEFINING MOMENTS IN BIDEN'S POLITICAL CAREER

1. Google Trends. "Search: Joe Biden." Accessed June 3, 2019.
2. "2008 Democratic Party Presidential Debates and Forums." Wikipedia. Last modified April 27, 2007. https://en.wikipedia.org/wiki/2008_Democratic _Party_presidential_debates_and_forums.
3. Nagourney, Adam, and Jeff Zeleny. "Obama Chooses Biden As Running Mate." *New York Times.* Last modified August 23, 2008. https://www .nytimes.com/2008/08/24/us/politics/24biden.html.
4. The Democratic Convention. "Transcript: Joe Biden's Acceptance Speech." NPR. Last modified August 27, 2008. https://www.npr.org/templates/story /story.php?storyId=94048033.
5. Rubin, Richard. "The Democrats Counted Correctly." *@PolitiFact.* Last modified August 28, 2008. https://www.politifact.com/truth-o-meter /statements/2008/aug/28/joe-biden/the-democrats-counted-correctly/.
6. DeCamp, David. "Biden Digs Back on Afghanistan to Dig McCain." *@PolitiFact.* Last modified August 28, 2008. https://www.politifact.com /truth-o-meter/statements/2008/aug/28/joe-biden/biden-digs-back-on -afghanistan-to-dig-mccain/.
7. "Dow Jones Industrial Average (^DJI) Stock Price, Quote, History & News." *Yahoo Finance.* Accessed June 3, 2019. https://finance.yahoo.com /quote/%5EDJI/.
8. U.S. Department of Labor. "Bureau of Labor Statistics Data." Accessed June 3, 2019.
9. Drawbaugh, Kevin, and Thomas Ferraro. "Angry White House Meeting Roils Bailout Talks." Reuters. Last modified September 26, 2008. https:// www.reuters.com/article/us-financial-bailout-mccain/angry-white-house -meeting-roils-bailout-talks-idUSTRE48P05S20080926?sp=true.
10. Election Center 2008. "Debate Poll Says Biden Won, Palin Beat Expectations.com." *CNN.* Accessed June 3, 2019. http://www.cnn.com /2008/POLITICS/10/03/debate.poll.index.html?eref=onion.
11. "Top 10 Joe Biden Gaffes." *TIME.* Last modified March 23, 2010. http:// content.time.com/time/specials/packages/article/0,28804,1895156 _1894977_1841630,00.html.
12. Hellerman, Caleb. "Democratic VP Nominee Biden Releases Medical Records.com." *CNN.* Accessed June 3, 2019. http://www.cnn.com/2008 /HEALTH/10/20/biden.health/.

13. "2008 United States Presidential Election." Wikipedia. Last modified December 18, 2003. https://en.wikipedia.org/wiki/2008_United_States _presidential_election.

14. "2016 United States Presidential Election." Wikipedia. Last modified February 3, 2009. https://en.wikipedia.org/wiki/2016_United_States _presidential_election.

15. Leibovich, Mark. "Speaking Freely, Biden Finds Influential Role." *New York Times.* Last modified March 28, 2009. https://www.nytimes.com /2009/03/29/us/politics/29biden.html.

16. "American Recovery and Reinvestment Act of 2009." Wikipedia. Last modified January 19, 2009. https://en.wikipedia.org/wiki/American_Recovery _and_Reinvestment_Act_of_2009.

17. Ibid.

18. Rodrigo, Chris M. "Sanders Leads Poll of Young Democrats by Double Digits." *The Hill.* Last modified April 1, 2019. https://thehill.com/homenews /campaign/436675-sanders-leads-poll-of-young-democratic-voters-by-double -digits.

19. Amadeo, Kimberly. "The Great Recession of 2008: What Happened, and When?" *The Balance.* Last modified June 23, 2016. https://www.thebalance .com/the-great-recession-of-2008-explanation-with-dates-4056832.

20. Lee, Carol E. "Biden Worked on Specter '100 Days.'" *Politico.* Last modified April 29, 2009. https://www.politico.com/story/2009/04/biden-worked -on-specter-100-days-021824.

21. Cohn, Jonathan. "How They Did It." *The New Republic.* Last modified May 21, 2010. https://newrepublic.com/article/75077/how-they-did-it.

22. "Patient Protection and Affordable Care Act." Wikipedia. Last modified November 28, 2009. https://en.wikipedia.org/wiki/Patient_Protection_and _Affordable_Care_Act.

23. Adams, Richard. "Joe Biden: 'This Is a Big Fucking Deal.'" *The Guardian.* Last modified July 18, 2017. https://www.theguardian.com/world/richard -adams-blog/2010/mar/23/joe-biden-obama-big-fucking-deal-overheard.

24. Traub, James. "Joe Biden: Second-Most Powerful Vice President in History?" *New York Times.* Last modified November 24, 2009. https:// www.nytimes.com/2009/11/29/magazine/29Biden-t.html.

25. "Vice President Biden: Iraq "Could Be One of the Great Achievements of This Administration."" *ABC News Blogs.* Accessed June 3, 2019. https:// web.archive.org/web/20150223113546/abcnews.go.com/blogs/politics/2010

/02/vice-president-biden-iraq-could-be-one-of-the-great-achievements-of
-this-administration/.

26. "Iraq Reinstates 59 Election Candidates." *Google News*. Last modified
January 25, 2010. https://web.archive.org/web/20130320192516/www.google
.com/hostednews/afp/article/ALeqM5iJGz55dJrnOzzejqmBj6QTolyydg.

27. Hasan, Mehdi, and Dina Sayedahmed. "Blowback: How ISIS Was Created
by the U.S. Invasion of Iraq." *The Intercept*. Last modified January 29, 2018.
https://theintercept.com/2018/01/29/isis-iraq-war-islamic-state-blowback/.

28. Lister, Charles. "Trump Says ISIS Is Defeated. Reality Says Otherwise."
Politico. Last modified March 18, 2019. https://www.politico.com/magazine
/story/2019/03/18/trump-isis-terrorists-defeated-foreign-policy-225816.

29. Liptak, Kevin. "Beau Biden, Son of VP Biden, Dies at 46Politics." CNN.
Last modified May 31, 2015. https://www.cnn.com/2015/05/30/politics
/obit-vice-president-son-beau-biden/index.html.

30. Barrish, Cris, and Jonathan Starkey. "Questions Remain About Beau
Biden's Health." *USA Today*. Last modified February 23, 2014. https://
www.usatoday.com/story/news/politics/2014/02/23/questions-remain-about
-beau-bidens-health/5733275/.

31. Matthews, Dylan. "Why Paul Manafort Pleaded Guilty to 'Conspiracy
Against the United States.'" *Vox*. Last modified March 13, 2019. https://
www.vox.com/2018/9/14/17860410/conspiracy-against-the-united-states
-paul-manafort-plea.

32. Osnos, Evan. "The Evolution of Joe Biden." *The New Yorker*. Last modified
July 20, 2014. https://www.newyorker.com/magazine/2014/07/28/biden
-agenda.

33. Ibid.

34. Liptak, Kevin. "Beau Biden, Son of VP Biden, Dies at 46." CNN. Last
modified May 31, 2015. https://www.cnn.com/2015/05/30/politics/obit-vice
-president-son-beau-biden/index.html.

35. Kane, Paul. "Beau Biden, vice president's son, dies at 46 of brain cancer."
Washington Post. Last modified May 31, 2015. https://www.washingtonpost
.com/politics/2015/05/30/e1ac5a2a-0731-11e5-a428-c984eb077d4e_story
.html?utm_term=.3a98b161227c.

36. "Biden Still Well-Liked by Americans." *Gallup*. Accessed June 4, 2019.
https://news.gallup.com/poll/247388/biden-liked-americans.aspx.

POLICY: CAMPAIGN PLATFORMS

1. "Joe's Vision." *Joe Biden for President 2020.* Last modified April 16, 2019. https://joebiden.com/joes-vision/.

2. "Education." *Joe Biden for President 2020.* Last modified May 28, 2019. https://joebiden.com/education/.

3. Kruzel, John. "Yes, Joe Biden Was a Climate Change Pioneer in Congress." *PolitiFact.* Last modified May 1, 2019. https://www.politifact.com/truth-o -meter/statements/2019/may/08/joe-biden/was-joe-biden-climate-change -pioneer-congress-hist/.

4. The 1994 crime bill issues are addressed at length in Chapter 8 of this book.

5. Williams, Sean. "Joe Biden Does an About-Face on Marijuana." *The Motley Fool.* Last modified May 25, 2019. https://www.fool.com/investing/2019/05 /25/joe-biden-does-an-about-face-on-marijuana.aspx.

6. Martin, Naomi, and James Pindell. "All 2020 Presidential Candidates Now Support Marijuana Legalization Efforts? Even the Republicans." *Boston Globe.* Last modified February 26, 2019. https://www.bostonglobe.com /news/marijuana/2019/02/26/all-presidential-candidates-support-legalizing -marijuana-even-republicans/bK4sQjPIgkzm54kl0dmZoI/story.html.

7. Bash, Dana. "Paul Ryan's New Partner: Obama." *CNN.* Last modified June 5, 2015. https://www.cnn.com/2015/06/05/politics/paul-ryan-trade -negotation-barack-obama/index.html.

BIOGRAPHY: BIDEN'S METEORIC RISE TO OFFICE AND HIS FAMILY TRAGEDY

1. Borys Krawczeniuk. "Remembering His Roots." *Scranton Times.* Last modified August 24, 2008. Accessed via the Wayback Machine May 30, 2019. https://web.archive.org/web/20090406014842/www.scrantontimes.com /articles/2008/08/24/news/sc_times_trib.20080824.a.pg1.tt24biden_s1 .1896121_top4.txt.

2. "Generations and Age." *Pew Research Center.* Last modified February 26, 2019. https://www.pewresearch.org/topics/generations-and-age/.

3. "Hunter Biden." Wikipedia. Last modified August 25, 2008. https:// en.wikipedia.org/wiki/Hunter_Biden.

4. "Our Staff & Board." *Delaware Center for Justice.* Accessed May 29, 2019. https://web.archive.org/web/20181025111906/www.dcjustice.org/staff-page/.

5. Rubinkam, Michael. "Biden's Scranton Childhood Left Lasting Impression." *Pittsburgh Post-Gazette.* Last modified August 27, 2008. https://www.post-gazette.com/news/politics-election-2008/2008/08/27/Biden-s-Scranton-childhood-left-lasting-impression/stories/200808270243.

6. "Edward Francis Blewitt." Wikipedia. Last modified April 27, 2019. https://en.wikipedia.org/wiki/Edward_Francis_Blewitt.

7. Smolenyak, Megan. "Joe Biden's Irish Roots." *Huffpost.* Last modified December 6, 2017. https://www.huffpost.com/entry/joe-bidens-irish-roots_b_1641678.

8. "Joe Biden: From Scranton to Vice President and Beyond." *Delaware News Journal.* Last modified January 4, 2019. https://www.delawareonline.com/story/news/politics/joe-biden/2019/01/04/joe-biden-scranton-vice-president-and-beyond/2480932002/.

9. Broder, John. "Father's Tough Life an Inspiration for Biden." *New York Times.* Last modified October 23, 2008. https://www.nytimes.com/2008/10/24/us/politics/24biden.html.

10. Political News. "Timeline of Biden's life and career." Associated Press. August 23, 2008. Accessed via Nexis.com 5/27/19.

11. Osnos, Evan. "The Evolution of Joe Biden." *The New Yorker.* Last modified July 20, 2014. https://www.newyorker.com/magazine/2014/07/28/biden-agenda.

12. "Joe Biden." *Biography.* Accessed May 29, 2019. https://www.biography.com/political-figure/joe-biden.

13. Kurtz, Howard. "Sen. Biden May Try to Talk His Way into the White House." *Washington Post.* July 28, 1987. https://www.washingtonpost.com/archive/politics/1986/07/28/sen-biden-may-try-to-talk-his-way-into-the-white-house/a19e4497-0d36-4536-95b7-abb38cc17888/.

14. Naylor, Brian. "Biden's Road to Senate Took Tragic Turn." NPR. Last modified October 8, 2007. https://www.npr.org/templates/story/story.php?storyId=14999603.

15. Kelley, Kitty. "Death and the All-American Boy." *Washingtonian.* Last modified March 5, 2019. https://www.washingtonian.com/1974/06/01/joe-biden-kitty-kelley-1974-profile-death-and-the-all-american-boy/.

16. "1972 United States Presidential Election in Delaware." Wikipedia. Last modified March 30, 2017. https://en.wikipedia.org/wiki/1972_United _States_presidential_election_in_Delaware.

17. Ibid.

18. Naylor, Brian. "Biden's Road to Senate Took Tragic Turn." NPR. Last modified October 8, 2007. https://www.npr.org/templates/story/story.php ?storyId=14999603.

19. Kruse M. "How Grief Became Joe Biden's 'Superpower.'" *Politico.* Last modified January 25, 2019. https://www.politico.com/magazine/story /2019/01/25/joe-biden-2019-profile-grief-beau-car-accident-224178.

EARLY SENATE CAREER

1. "Sen. BIDEN, Joseph Robinette, Jr. (Democrat, DE): Sen. BIDEN is More Liberal Than 65 percent of the 111th Congress, and More Conservative Than 57 percent of Democrats." *Vote view.* Accessed June 1, 2019. https:// voteview.com/person/14101/joseph-robinette-biden-jr.

2. Kruzel, John. "Biden Says He Was a Staunchly Liberal Senator. He Wasn't." *PolitiFact.* Last modified May 1, 2019. https://www.politifact.com/truth-o -meter/statements/2019/may/06/joe-biden/joe-biden-claims-he-was-staunch -liberal-senate-he-/.

3. National Journal. "Biden's Senate Vote Record." Wayback Machine. Accessed June 1, 2019. https://web.archive.org/web/20090408054840 /www.nationaljournal.com:80/conventions/co_20080823_9669.php.

4. Cramer, Richard Ben. "What It Takes: The Way To The White House." 2011. Newburyport: Open Road Media.

5. Wilser, Jeff. *The Book of Joe.* New York: Three Rivers Press, 2017.

6. Kruse, Michael. "How Grief Became Joe Biden's 'Superpower." *Politico.* Last modified January 25, 2019. https://www.politico.com/magazine/story /2019/01/25/joe-biden-2019-profile-grief-beau-car-accident-224178.

7. "Joe Biden: From Scranton to Vice President and Beyond." *Delaware News Journal.* Last modified January 4, 2019. https://www.delawareonline.com /story/news/politics/joe-biden/2019/01/04/joe-biden-scranton-vice-president -and-beyond/2480932002/.

8. "U.S. Senate: Youngest Senator." U.S. Senate. Last modified January 24, 2019. https://www.senate.gov/artandhistory/history/minute/Youngest _Senator.htm.

9. Ungar, Sanford. "The Man Who Runs the Senate." *The Atlantic.* Accessed June 1, 2019. https://www.theatlantic.com/magazine/archive/1975/09/the -man-who-runs-the-senate/308168/.

10. Dwyer, Devin. "Biden Reflects on Immense Grief After Loss of Wife, Daughter." ABC News. Accessed June 1, 2019. https://abcnews.go.com/blogs /politics/2012/05/joe-biden-reflects-on-grief-suicidal-thoughts-after-death -of-wife-and-daughter/.

11. Kelley, Kitty. "Death and the All-American Boy." *Washingtonian.* Last modified March 5, 2019. https://washingtonian.com/1974/06/01/joe-biden -kitty-kelley-1974-profile-death-and-the-all-american-boy/.

12. Bluestone, Gabrielle. "Here's That Anti-Semitic Joke Joe Biden Tried to Keep Off the Record." *Gawker.* Accessed June 1, 2019. http://gawker.com /heres-that-antisemetic-joke-joe-biden-tried-to-keep-of-1734751552.

13. "CONGRESSIONAL RECORD-SENATE." *Govinfo | U.S. Government Publishing Office.* Last modified September 5, 1974. https://www.govinfo .gov/content/pkg/GPO-CRECB-1974-pt23/pdf/GPO-CRECB-1974-pt23 -2-1.pdf.

14. Seelye, Katharine. "Jill Biden Heads toward Life in the Spotlight." *New York Times.* Last modified August 24, 2008. https://www.nytimes.com /2008/08/25/us/politics/25wife.html.

15. Collins, Nancy. "The Gossip Column." *Washington Post.* June 22, 1977. Via Nexis.com accessed May 31, 2019.

16. Sokol, Jason. "How a Young Joe Biden Turned Liberals Against Integration." *Politico.* Last modified August 4, 2015. https://www.politico .com/magazine/story/2015/08/joe-biden-integration-school-busing -120968?o=1.

17. UPI. "Antibusing Measure Approved In Senate." *New York Times.* Last modified September 18, 1975. https://www.nytimes.com/1975/09/18 /archives/anti-busing-measure-approved-in-senate.html.

18. Goodman, Alana. "Joe Biden Embraced Segregation in 1975, Claiming It Was a Matter of 'Black Pride.'" *Washington Examiner.* Last modified February 1, 2019. https://www.washingtonexaminer.com/politics/joe-biden -embraced-segregation-in-1975-claiming-it-was-a-matter-of-black-pride.

19. Viser, Matt. "Biden's tough talk on 1970s school desegregation plan could get new scrutiny in today's Democratic Party." *Washington Post.* Last modified March 7, 2019. https://www.washingtonpost.com/politics/bidens-tough -talk-on-1970s-school-desegregation-plan-could-get-new-scrutiny-in-todays-democratic-party/2019/03/07/9115583e-3eb2-11e9-a0d3-1210e58a94cf _story.html?utm_term=.17dca4cd93ab.

20. Ordovensky, Pat. "Biden on busing: Don't learn how to hate." *Wilmington Evening Journal.* November 24, 1976. Accessed June 2, 2019. https://www .documentcloud.org/documents/5798659-Biden-76.html.

21. Viser, Matt. "Biden's tough talk on 1970s school desegregation plan could get new scrutiny in today's Democratic Party." *Washington Post.* Last modified March 7, 2019. https://www.washingtonpost.com/politics/bidens-tough -talk-on-1970s-school-desegregation-plan-could-get-new-scrutiny-in-todays -democratic-party/2019/03/07/9115583e-3eb2-11e9-a0d3-1210e58a94cf _story.html?utm_term=.17dca4cd93ab.

22. Schram, Martin. "Candidates Bask in the Warm Air of Endorsements." *Washington Post.* Last modified November 2, 1979. https://www .washingtonpost.com/archive/politics/1979/11/02/candidates-bask-in-the -warm-air-of-endorsements/7f62caa0-7e23-477d-b79c-26edcc867cca/?utm _term=.c9d6ccb14cc4.

23. "United States Senate Committee on Foreign Relations." Wikipedia. Last modified February 12, 2004. https://en.wikipedia.org/wiki/United_States _Senate_Committee_on_Foreign_Relations.

24. "Church Committee." Wikipedia. Last modified December 7, 2004. https://en.wikipedia.org/wiki/Church_Committee.

25. Lardner Jr., George. "Biden Disturbed by Possible Precedent of Helms Case." *Washington Post.* Last modified November 15, 1977. https://www .washingtonpost.com/archive/politics/1977/11/15/biden-disturbed-by -possible-precedent-of-helms-case/7f21d698-2ae8-4a8f-8648-8f8d574905f1 /?utm_term=.b6efd7e08296.

26. Thornton, Mary. "Senate Unit Narrows Bill on Naming U.S. Agents." *Washington Post.* Last modified October 7, 1981. https://www .washingtonpost.com/archive/politics/1981/10/07/senate-unit-narrows-bill -on-naming-us-agents/737dfd65-d217-4688-b37d-dabfa34b9752/?utm _term=.e0be99dae4b4.

27. Gordon, Michael R. "In Biden, Obama Chooses a Foreign Policy Adherent of Diplomacy before Force." *New York Times.* Last modified August 24,

2008. https://www.nytimes.com/2008/08/24/world/americas/24iht-policy
.4.15591832.html.

28. "Strategic Defense Initiative." Wikipedia. Last modified December 10,
2001. https://en.wikipedia.org/wiki/Strategic_Defense_Initiative.

29. Atlas, Terry. "Shultz Blistered on S. Africa." *Chicago Tribune.* Last modified
September 4, 2018. https://www.chicagotribune.com/news/ct-xpm-1986-07
-24-8602230193-story.html.

30. LeTourneau, Nancy. "Toward a More Balanced View of Joe Biden's Legacy."
Washington Monthly. Last modified March 8, 2019. https://washingtonmonthly
.com/2019/03/08/towards-a-more-balanced-view-of-joe-bidens-legacy/.

31. It was revealed shortly after Sen. Thurmond's death that he had a secret
daughter with an African American woman.

32. Maitland, Leslie. "U.S. Plans A New Drive On Narcotics." *New York Times.*
Last modified October 9, 1982. https://www.nytimes.com/1982/10/09/us
/us-plans-a-new-drive-on-narcotics.html.

33. Kurtz, Howard. "Sen. Biden May Try to Talk His Way Into the White
House." *Washington Post.* Last modified July 27, 1986. https://www
.washingtonpost.com/archive/politics/1986/07/28/sen-biden-may-try-to
-talk-his-way-into-the-white-house/a19e4497-0d36-4536-95b7
-abb38cc17888/?utm_term=.c0f5d4050570.

34. "Comprehensive Crime Control Act of 1984." Wikipedia. Last modified
April 14, 2012. https://en.wikipedia.org/wiki/Comprehensive_Crime
_Control_Act_of_1984.

35. Rudin, Ken. "Specter Helped Defeat Sessions In 1986 Judiciary Vote."
NPR. Last modified May 5, 2009. https://www.npr.org/sections
/politicaljunkie/2009/05/specter_helped_defeat_sessions.html.

36. Kurtz, Howard. "Sen Biden May Try to Talk His Way Into the White
House." *Washington Post.* Last modified July 28, 1986. https://www
.washingtonpost.com/archive/politics/1986/07/28/sen-biden-may-try-to
-talk-his-way-into-the-white-house/a19e4497-0d36-4536-95b7
-abb38cc17888/?utm_term=.c0f5d4050570.

37. "1986 United States Elections." Wikipedia. Last modified June 24, 2009.
https://en.wikipedia.org/wiki/1986_United_States_elections.

SENATOR BIDEN'S FIRST PRESIDENTIAL RUN AND THE BORK HEARINGS

1. Dionne, E. J., Jr. "Biden Joins Campaign for the Presidency." *New York Times.* Last modified June 10, 1987. https://www.nytimes.com/1987/06/10 /us/biden-joins-campaign-for-the-presidency.html.

2. Kamen, Al. "Justice Powell Resigns, Was Supreme Court's Pivotal Vote." *Washington Post.* Last modified June 27, 1987. https://www.washingtonpost .com/wp-srv/national/longterm/supcourt/stories/powell062787.htm.

3. Fuerbringer, Jonathan. "Byrd Says Bork Nomination Would Face Senate Trouble." *New York Times.* Last modified June 30, 1987. https://www .nytimes.com/1987/06/30/us/byrd-says-bork-nomination-would-face -senate-trouble.html.

4. Cannon, Lou, and Edward Walsh. "Reagan Nominates Appeals Judge Bork To Supreme Court." *Washington Post.* Last modified July 2, 1987. https:// www.washingtonpost.com/archive/politics/1987/07/02/reagan-nominates -appeals-judge-bork-to-supreme-court/de36535e-e75e-435f-8686 -51b18db345c6/?utm_term=.a0f80ce52743.

5. "Saturday Night Massacre." Wikipedia. Last modified October 19, 2003. https://en.wikipedia.org/wiki/Saturday_Night_Massacre.

6. "Senate Judiciary Committee plans 10 Days of Hearings on Bork Nomination." Associated Press. August 5, 1987. Accessed via Nexis.com June 1, 2019.

7. Glover, Mike. "Biden Juggles Presidential Bid and Judiciary Chairmanship." Associated Press. August 24, 1987. Accessed via Nexis.com on June 1, 2019.

8. UPI. "Biden Report Says White House Has Skewed Bork Image." *Los Angeles Times.* September 3, 1987.

9. Dowd, Maureen. "Biden's Debate Finale: An Echo from Abroad." *New York Times.* Last modified September 12, 1987. https://www.nytimes.com /1987/09/12/us/biden-s-debate-finale-an-echo-from-abroad.html.

10. Skorneck, Carolyn. "Biden Aide Says Non-Attribution of Speech to British Politician Not Intended." Associated Press. September 12, 1987. Accessed via Nexis.com on June 1, 2019.

11. Skorneck, Carolyn. "Biden Feels Reports Over Unattributed Speech 'Go With The Territory.'" Associated Press. September 13, 1987. Accessed via Nexis.com on June 1, 2019.

12. Skorneck, Carolyn. "Biden Aides Say Reports Over Unattributed Speech Won't Affect Campaign." Associated Press. September 14, 1987. Accessed via Nexis.com on June 1, 2019.

13. Harwood, John. "Senate hearings put Biden in spotlight." *St. Petersburg Times.* September 15, 1987. Accessed via Nexis.com June 1, 2019.

14. Schwartz, Maralee. "Biden Faces Second Round of Plagiarism Accusations." *Washington Post.* September 16, 1998. Accessed via Nexis.com June 1, 2019.

15. Dionne, E. J. "Biden Was Accused of Plagiarism in Law School." *New York Times.* September 17, 1987.

16. Dionne, E. J. "Biden Admits Plagiarism in School But Says It Was Not 'Malevolent.'" *New York Times.* September 18, 1987.

17. Russakoff, Dale. "Senate Judiciary Committee Rallies behind Its Chairman." *Washington Post.* September 18, 1987.

18. Warren, Ellen and Epstein, Aaron. "Bork Grilled By Skeptics on Sincerity." *The Miami Herald.* September 19, 1987.

19. Witt, Evans. "Biden Claimed He Was In Top Half Of Law Class." Associated Press. September 21, 1987. Accessed via Nexis.com on June 1, 2019.

20. Rothenberg, Donald M. "Democrats Fear Permanent Taint From Hart, Biden Problems." Associated Press. September 23, 1987. Accessed via Nexis.com June 1, 2019.

21. Donald M. Rothenberg. "Biden Has Solace in Judiciary Chairmanship." Associated Press. September 23, 1987. Accessed via Nexis.com June 1, 2019.

22. Wire Report. "Biden's GOP Challenger Dusts off Plagiarism Controversy in Videotapes." Associated Press. October 10, 1990. Accessed via Nexis.com June 1, 2019.

23. 1990 United States Senate Election in Delaware." Wikipedia. Last modified November 9, 2012. https://en.wikipedia.org/wiki/1990_United_States_Senate_election_in_Delaware.

24. Dionne, E.J. "Biden Withdraws Bid for President in Wake of Furor.'" *New York Times.* September 24, 1987.

25. Rubin, James H. "Bork Hearings End; Carter Urges Rejection." Associated Press. September 30, 1987. Accessed via Nexis.com June 1, 2019.

26. "Dukakis Says His Campaign Chief Helped Topple Biden; 2 Aides Quit After Gov.'s Disclosure." *Los Angeles Times* September 30, 1987. Accessed via Nexis.com June 1, 2019.

27. Taylor, Paul. "Democrats Differ On Harm To Dukakis Campaign." *Washington Post.* Last modified October 1, 1987. https://www.washingtonpost.com/archive/politics/1987/10/01/democrats-differ-on-harm-to-dukakis-campaign/61f1c3dd-a3f1-455f-a578-c340131e373c/?utm_term=.34a8a564c819.

28. "Willie Horton." Wikipedia. Last modified February 7, 2004. https://en.wikipedia.org/wiki/Willie_Horton.

29. "Panel Rejects Bork 9 to 5; Reagan Refuses to give up: Sen. Heflin Casts Vote with Foes." *Los Angeles Times.* Last modified March 12, 2019. https://www.latimes.com/archives/la-xpm-1987-10-06-mn-12517-story.html.

30. "53 Senators against Bork, 36 for Him in AP Headcount." Associated Press. October 10, 1990. Accessed via Nexis.com June 1, 2019.

31. Margasak, Larry. "Senate Opens Debate on Bork Nomination, Defeat Virtually Certain." Associated Press. October 21, 1987. Accessed via Nexis.com June 1, 2019.

32. Margasak, Larry. "Senate Rejects Bork Nomination by Record 58–42 Vote." Associated Press. October 23, 1987. Accessed via Nexis.com June 1, 2019.

33. "Bork Battle May Have Permanently Altered Senate Confirmation Process." Associated Press. October 26, 1987. Accessed via Nexis.com June 1, 2019.

34. Taylor, Stuart Jr. "Baker Meets Key Senate Democrats to Discuss Possible Nominees to Court." *New York Times.* Last modified October 28, 1987. https://www.nytimes.com/1987/10/28/us/baker-meets-key-senate-democrats-to-discuss-possible-nominees-to-court.html.

35. Rubin, James H. "Senate Votes 97–0 to Confirm Kennedy for Supreme Court." Associated Press. February 3, 1988. Accessed via Nexis.com June 1, 2019.

36. Newman, Meredith. "What Joe Biden Learned from His Life-threatening Brain Aneurysms." *Delaware online.* Last modified March 18, 2019. https://www.delawareonline.com/story/news/politics/joe-biden/2019/03/18/joe-biden-2020-how-then-senator-overcame-life-threatening-brain-aneurysms/3002961002/.

37. Biden, Joseph R. "Promises To Keep." 2008. New York: Random House Trade Paperbacks.

LATE SENATE CAREER

1. "Liberal Justice Brennan, 84, Retires From Supreme Court; Resignation: President Bush Will Get Chance To Make His First High Court Appointment. A Dramatic Shift In Liberal-Conservative Balance Is Bound To Occur." *Los Angeles Times*. July 22, 1990. Accessed via Nexis.com June 1, 2019.

2. "PN1414 - Nomination of David H. Souter for Supreme Court of the United States, 101st Congress (1989–1990)." Congress.gov. Last modified October 2, 1990. https://www.congress.gov/nomination/101st-congress /1414.

3. "Kuwait–United States Relations." Wikipedia. Last modified February 27, 2008. https://en.wikipedia.org/wiki/Kuwait%E2%80%93United_States _relations.

4. "Hearing Of The Senate Foreign Relations Committee Subject: U.S. Policy In The Persian Gulf Chaired By: Senator Joseph Biden (D-De)." Federal News Service. December 12, 1990. Accessed via Nexis.com on June 2, 2019.

5. Arango, Tim. "Iraqi Shiite Anger at U.S. Remains Strong." *New York Times*. Last modified November 8, 2011. https://www.nytimes.com/2011/11/09 /world/middleeast/iraqi-shiite-anger-at-united-states-remains-strong.html.

6. Diebe, Lindal. "Congress mood grim as Gulf War debated." *Toronto Star*. January 11, 1991. Accessed via Nexis.com on June 2, 2019.

7. "United States Senate Debate: S.J. Res. 1 - Mitchell/Nunn Speaker: Senator Joseph Biden, Jr., D-De." Federal News Service. January 12, 1991. Accessed via Nexis.com on June 2, 2019.

8. "Authorization for Use of Military Force against Iraq Resolution of 1991." Wikipedia. Last modified November 20, 2007. https://en.wikipedia.org/ wiki/Authorization_for_Use_of_Military_Force_Against_Iraq_Resolution _of_1991.

9. Beardsley, Steven. "'Mother of All Battles' Lasted Only 100 Hours." *Stars and Stripes*. Accessed June 3, 2019. https://www.stripes.com/news/special -reports/the-gulf-war-25-year-anniversary/100-hours.

10. Gordon, Michael R. "A Democratic Leader on Foreign Policy, in Iraq and the Balkans." *New York Times*. Last modified August 23, 2008. https:// www.nytimes.com/2008/08/24/us/politics/24policy.html.

11. Congress.gov. "PN838 - Nomination of Clarence Thomas for the Judiciary, 101st Congress (1989–1990)." *Congress.gov*. Last modified March 6, 1990. https://www.congress.gov/nomination/101st-congress/838.

12. "Clarence Thomas Supreme Court Nomination." Wikipedia. Last modified November 9, 2007. https://en.wikipedia.org/wiki/Clarence_Thomas_Supreme_Court_nomination#Nomination.

13. "NOW to Fight Confirmation of Thomas: Supreme Court: The Women's Rights Organization Calls Bush's Nominee an 'extremist.' 'We're going to Bork Him,' Says One of Its Lawyers." *Los Angeles Times*. Last modified March 9, 2019. https://www.latimes.com/archives/la-xpm-1991-07-06-mn-1560-story.html.

14. Kelleher, Paul J. "Neil Gorsuch's "Natural Law" Philosophy is a Long Way from Justice Scalia's Originalism." *Vox*. Last modified March 20, 2017. https://www.vox.com/the-big-idea/2017/3/20/14976926/gorsuch-natural-law-supreme-court-hearings.

15. LaFraniere, Sharon. "Despite achievement, Thomas felt isolated." *Washington Post*. Last modified September 9, 1991. https://www.washingtonpost.com/archive/politics/1991/09/09/despite-achievement-thomas-felt-isolated/fa807e3d-4664-4ea4-a170-c52070850894/?utm_term=.00091cab44a4.

16. Totenberg, Nina. "NPR's Nina Totenberg Recalls Breaking Anita Hill's Story In 1991." NPR. Last modified April 14, 2016. https://www.npr.org/2016/04/14/474265633/nprs-nina-totenberg-recalls-breaking-anita-hills-story-in-1991.

17. Totenberg, Nina. "A Timeline of Clarence Thomas–Anita Hill Controversy as Kavanaugh to Face Accuser." NPR. Last modified September 23, 2018. https://www.npr.org/2018/09/23/650138049/a-timeline-of-clarence-thomas-anita-hill-controversy-as-kavanaugh-to-face-accuse.

18. Raymond, Adam. "A Brief Guide to the Joe Biden 'Anita Hill Controversy.'" *Intelligencer*. Last modified May 7, 2019. http://nymag.com/intelligencer/2019/05/guide-joe-biden-anita-hill-controversy.html.

19. Klein, Asher. "Biden on Hill Hearings: 'What the Devil Have We Learned?'" NBC New York. Last modified September 21, 2018. https://www.nbcnewyork.com/news/politics/Biden-Anita-Hill-Apology-Ford-Kavanaugh-493938191.html.

20. Stolberg, Sheryl Gay. "Excerpts from Anita Hill's Interview with the Times." *New York Times*. Last modified April 28, 2019. https://www

.nytimes.com/2019/04/26/us/politics/clarence-thomas-anita-hill-joe-biden
.html?module=inline.

21. "Year of the Woman." Wikipedia. Last modified September 23, 2005.
https://en.wikipedia.org/wiki/Year_of_the_Woman.

22. "Civil Rights Act of 1991." Wikipedia. Last modified February 15, 2005.
https://en.wikipedia.org/wiki/Civil_Rights_Act_of_1991.

23. Fandos, Nicholas. "Joe Biden's Role in '90s Crime Law Could Haunt Any
Presidential Bid." *New York Times.* Last modified January 19, 2018. https://
www.nytimes.com/2015/08/22/us/politics/joe-bidens-role-in-90s-crime-law
-could-haunt-any-presidential-bid.html.

24. "Violent Crime Control and Law Enforcement Act." Wikipedia. Last modified April 22, 2003. https://en.wikipedia.org/wiki/Violent_Crime_Control
_and_Law_Enforcement_Act.

25. Ifill, Gwen. "White House Offers Version of Three-Strike Crime Bill." *New
York Times.* Last modified March 2, 1994. https://www.nytimes.com/1994
/03/02/us/white-house-offers-version-of-three-strikes-crime-bill.html.

26. "United States Incarceration Rate." Wikipedia. Last modified May 1, 2008.
https://en.wikipedia.org/wiki/United_States_incarceration_rate.

27. Ingraham, Christopher. "The U.S. has more jails than colleges. Here's a
map of where those prisoners live." *Washington Post.* Last modified January
6, 2015. https://www.washingtonpost.com/news/wonk/wp/2015/01/06/the
-u-s-has-more-jails-than-colleges-heres-a-map-of-where-those-prisoners-live
/?utm_term=.9d885ba7354a.

28. NCJRS. "Violent Crime Control and Law Enforcement Act of 1994."
National Criminal Justice Reference Service. Accessed June 3, 2019. https://
www.ncjrs.gov/txtfiles/billfs.txt.

29. Lopez, German. "If Joe Biden Runs for President, He's Going to Have a Big
Problem with Black Lives Matter." *Vox.* Last modified August 26, 2015.
https://www.vox.com/2015/8/26/9208983/joe-biden-black-lives-matter.

30. "Text of S. 1711 (110th): Drug Sentencing Reform and Cocaine Kingpin
Trafficking Act of 2007 (Introduced Version)." GovTrack.us. Accessed June
3, 2019. https://www.govtrack.us/congress/bills/110/s1711/text/is.

31. "Fair Sentencing Act." Wikipedia. Last modified August 5, 2010. https://
en.wikipedia.org/wiki/Fair_Sentencing_Act.

32. "U.S. Sentencing Commission Reports on Impact of Fair Sentencing Act of
2010: Finds Decline in Federal Crack Cocaine Prosecutions." United States
Sentencing Commission. Last modified August 3, 2015. https://www.ussc

.gov/sites/default/files/pdf/news/press-releases-and-news-advisories/press
-releases/20150803_Press_Release.pdf.

33. National Reentry Resource Center. "Second Chance Act Grant Program."
    CSG Justice Center. Accessed June 3, 2019. http://csgjusticecenter.org/nrrc
    /projects/second-chance-act/.

34. Thayer, Kate. "The Violence Against Women Act Has Expired. Advocates
    Say That Sends a Dangerous Message and Are Pushing for Permanent
    Protections." *Chicago Tribune.* Last modified February 21, 2019. https://
    www.chicagotribune.com/lifestyles/ct-life-violence-against-women-act
    -expired-20190220-story.html.

35. Shabad, Rebecca. "House Votes to Reauthorize Violence against Women
    Act, Despite GOP Opposition." NBC News. Last modified April 4, 2019.
    https://www.nbcnews.com/politics/congress/house-votes-reauthorize
    -violence-against-women-act-despite-gop-opposition-n990931.

36. Haley, Grace, and Evers-Hillstrom, Karl. "NRA Opposition Upsets Effort to
    Reauthorize Expired Violence Against Women Act." *OpenSecrets News.* Last
    modified March 28, 2019. https://www.opensecrets.org/news/2019/03/nra
    -opposition-upsets-effort-to-reauthorize-expired-violence-against-women
    -act/.

37. "S.226 - 108th Congress (2003–2004): Illicit Drug Anti-Proliferation Act
    of 2003." *Congress.gov.* Last modified April 10, 2003. https://www.congress
    .gov/bill/108th-congress/senate-bill/226.

38. "DEA Must Not Be Allowed to Chill Speech or Shut Down Electronic
    Music Events." *American Civil Liberties Union.* Accessed June 3, 2019.
    https://www.aclu.org/other/dea-must-not-be-allowed-chill-speech-or-shut
    -down-electronic-music-events.

39. "Why Incorporate in Delaware or Nevada?" *Bizfilings.* Accessed June 3,
    2019. https://www.bizfilings.com/toolkit/research-topics/incorporating
    -your-business/why-incorporate-in-delaware-or-nevada.

40. Meyer, Theodoric. "Inside Biden and Warren's Years long Feud." *Politico.*
    Last modified March 12, 2019. https://www.politico.com/magazine/story
    /2019/03/12/biden-vs-warren-2020-democratic-primaries-bankruptcy-bill
    -225728.

41. Morgan, Dan. "Money Talks Louder in Bankruptcy Debate." *Washington
    Post.* Last modified June 1, 1999. https://www.washingtonpost.com/archive
    /politics/1999/06/01/creditors-money-talks-louder-in-bankruptcy-debate
    /dde6db41-2874-4ef7-9442-3fff5b7e9401/?utm_term=.f2c3c27f3aed.

42. Meyer, Theodoric. "Inside Biden and Warren's Years long Feud." *Politico.* Last modified March 12, 2019. https://www.politico.com/magazine/story /2019/03/12/biden-vs-warren-2020-democratic-primaries-bankruptcy -bill-225728.

43. Przybyla, Heidi. "Joe Biden's Record Could Pose Difficulties for 2016 White House Bid." *USA TODAY.* Last modified September 30, 2015. https://www.usatoday.com/story/news/politics/elections/2015/09/30/joe -biden-senate-record-2016-campaign/73045484/.

44. Crowley, Michael. "Rhetorical Question." *The New Republic.* Last modified October 22, 2001. https://newrepublic.com/article/61756/rhetorical -question.

45. Gordon, Michael R. "A Democratic Leader on Foreign Policy, in Iraq and the Balkans." *New York Times.* Last modified August 23, 2008. https:// www.nytimes.com/2008/08/24/us/politics/24policy.html.

46. Zunes, Stephen. "The Other Reason Biden Shouldn't Run." *Common Dreams.* Last modified April 2, 2019. https://www.commondreams.org /views/2019/04/02/other-reason-biden-shouldnt-run?fbclid=IwAR04bkZ _EcuA2rj3O-tlG78LoPUPYsR8QKJT5ZCJNFfQ_hcOQOyj1v9RBWA.

47. "Joe Biden Iraq War." C-SPAN.org. October 10, 2002. https://www.c-span. org/video/?c4757852/joe-biden-iraq-war.

48. Haltiwanger, John. "Bernie Sanders Revisits His Vote Against the Iraq War, Which Started 16 Years Ago Today, and Says Much of What He Feared Came True." *Business Insider.* Last modified March 20, 2019. https://www .businessinsider.com/bernie-sanders-revisits-vote-against-iraq-war-16th -anniversary-invasion-2019-3.

49. Congress.gov. "Actions - H.J.Res.114 - 107th Congress (2001–2002): Authorization for Use of Military Force against Iraq Resolution of 2002." *Congress.gov.* Last modified October 16, 2002. https://www.congress.gov /bill/107th-congress/house-joint-resolution/114/actions.

50. Breslow, Jason. "Colin Powell: U.N. Speech 'Was a Great Intelligence Failure.'" *FRONTLINE.* Last modified May 17, 2016. https://www.pbs.org /wgbh/frontline/article/colin-powell-u-n-speech-was-a-great-intelligence -failure/.

51. "White House Iraq Group." Wikipedia. Last modified July 21, 2005. https://en.wikipedia.org/wiki/White_House_Iraq_Group.

52. Goldsmith, Jack. "The 2002 Iraq AUMF Almost Certainly Authorizes the President to Use Force Today in Iraq (and Might Authorize the Use of Force

in Syria) [UPDATED]." *Lawfare.* Last modified June 10, 2015. https://www.lawfareblog.com/2002-iraq-aumf-almost-certainly-authorizes-president-use-force-today-iraq-and-might-authorize-use.

53. "Coalition Provisional Authority Order 2." Wikipedia. Last modified January 26, 2008. https://en.wikipedia.org/wiki/Coalition_Provisional_Authority_Order_2.

54. "U.S. Senate: U.S. Senate Roll Call Votes 110th Congress - 1st Session." *U.S. Senate.* Last modified May 31, 2019. https://www.senate.gov/legislative/LIS/roll_call_lists/roll_call_vote_cfm.cfm?congress=110&session=1&vote=00348.

55. Gerstein, Josh. "Was Biden Right?" *Politico.* Last modified June 15, 2014. https://www.politico.com/story/2014/06/joe-biden-iraq-107858.

56. Madej, Patricia. "This Isn't Joe Biden's First Run at President. Here's How He Launched His Past Campaigns." *Inquirer.* Last modified April 25, 2019. https://www.inquirer.com/politics/nation/joe-biden-presidential-campaign-launch-history-1988-2008-20190425.html.

57. Sawyer, Diane. "Biden Runs for White House; 'I'm the 880th Candidate." *Good Morning America.* ABC. January 31, 2007. Accessed via Nexis.com on June 2, 2019.

58. Balz, Dan. "Biden Stumbles at the Starting Gate Comments About Obama Overtake Bid for President." *Washington Post.* Last modified February 1, 2007. www.washingtonpost.com/wp-dyn/content/article/2007/01/31/AR2007013100404.html.

59. "Joe's Right . . . ." *Democratic Underground.* Accessed June 3, 2019. https://www.democraticunderground.org/128797211.

60. Halperin, Mark, and John Heilemann. *Game Change.* HarperCollins. 2010. New York, NY.

61. Smith, Ben. "A Noun, a Verb, and 9/11 . . . ." *Politico.* Last modified October 30, 2007. https://www.politico.com/blogs/ben-smith/2007/10/a-noun-a-verb-and-9-11-003927.

62. Glover, Mike. "Biden Bets on Iowa to Boost Candidacy." *Washington Post.* September 7, 2007. www.washingtonpost.com/wp-dyn/content/article/2007/09/03/AR2007090300127_2.html.

63. "2008 Iowa Democratic Caucuses." Wikipedia. Last modified November 11, 2006. https://en.wikipedia.org/wiki/2008_Iowa_Democratic_caucuses.

ANALYSIS OF JOE BIDEN'S CHANCES FOR WINNING THE NOMINATION AND PRESIDENCY

1. Glueck, Katie. "Biden Delivers Call for National Unity at Philadelphia Rally." *New York Times.* Last modified May 19, 2019. https://www.nytimes .com/2019/05/18/us/politics/joe-biden-philadelphia-rally.html.

2. Morin, Rebecca. "Biden Quickly Raises $6.3 Million, Marking the Largest 24-hour Haul from 2020 Candidates." *USA TODAY.* Last modified April 26, 2019. https://www.usatoday.com/story/news/politics/elections/2019/04 /26/joe-biden-campaign-money-2020-election/3589957002/.

3. Caputo, Marc, and Scott Bland. "Biden Crushes It in First-day fundraising: $6.3 Million." *Politico.* Last modified April 26, 2019. https://www.politico .com/story/2019/04/26/biden-fundraising-numbers-2020-1291180.

4. Biden, Joe. *Twitter.* Accessed June 3, 2019. https://twitter.com/JoeBiden /status/1121915023444590601.

5. Jennifer Rubin, interviewed by author, May 17, 2019.

6. Stein, Jeff. "Bring it on': Biden and Sanders teams kick off debate over Medicare-for-all." *Washington Post.* Last modified April 29, 2019. https:// www.washingtonpost.com/us-policy/2019/04/29/bring-it-biden-sanders -teams-kick-off-debate-over-medicare-for-all/.

7. Davenport, Coral, and Katie Glueck. "Joe Biden Issue Climate Plan that Aims Beyond Obama's Goal." *New York Times.* June 4, 2019. https://www .nytimes.com/2019/06/04/us/politics/joe-biden-climate-plan.html?smid =nytcore-ios-share

8. "Democratic Presidential Candidate Joe Biden Gives Campaign Rally Speech in Philadelphia, Pennsylvania." CNN Newsroom. May 18, 2019.

9. Rubin, Jennifer. "Dear GOP: I'm just not that into you." *Washington Post.* May 16, 2016. https://www.washingtonpost.com/blogs/right-turn/wp/2016 /05/16/dear-gop-im-just-not-that-into-you/?utm_term=.abd58ba63b14.

10. "Democratic Dividing Lines." *Echelon Insights.* Last modified May 20, 2019. http://echeloninsights.com/wp-content/uploads/Omnibus-May-2019_Dem -Primary.pdf.

11. Rubin, Jennifer. "When the field thins, Joe Biden still may be on top." *Washington Post.* Last modified May 28, 2019. https://www.washingtonpost .com/opinions/2019/05/28/when-field-thins-biden-still-may-be-top/?utm _term=.e8733ffce3c8

12. "Election 2020 - 2020 Democratic Presidential Nomination." *RealClearPolitics*. Accessed June 3, 2019. https://www.realclearpolitics.com /epolls/2020/president/us/2020_democratic_presidential_nomination -6730.html#polls.

13. Kamisar, Ben. "Biden with Big Lead in New Hampshire Poll." *NBC News*. Accessed June 3, 2019. https://www.nbcnews.com/card/biden-big-lead-new -hampshire-poll-n1003846.

14. Pindell, James. "Biden, Followed by Sanders and Buttigieg, Leads Among Democrats in N.H. Survey." *Boston Globe*. Last modified April 29, 2019. https://www2.bostonglobe.com/metro/2019/04/29/biden-followed-sanders -and-buttigieg-lead-among-democrats-survey/Gs0gireOuJxvw5SfTTy5wM /story.html.

15. "Election 2020 - Iowa Democratic Presidential Caucus." *RealClearPolitics*. Accessed June 3, 2019. https://www.realclearpolitics.com/epolls/2020 /president/ia/iowa_democratic_presidential_caucus-6731.html.

16. Bycoffe, Aaron, Ritchie King, and Dhrumil Mehta. "Iowa President: Democratic Primary Polls." FiveThirtyEight. Last modified June 28, 2018. https://projects.fivethirtyeight.com/polls/president-primary-d/iowa/.

17. Emerson polling. "Wisconsin 2020: Bernie Sanders Leads Democratic Field; Trump Competitive in General Election." *Reportable*. Accessed June 3, 2019. https://emersonpolling.reportablenews.com/pr/wisconsin-2020 -bernie-sanders-leads-democratic-field-trump-competitive-in-general -election.

18. Shain, Andy. "'The Safe Choice:' Biden Widens SC Lead in 2020 Democratic Presidential Primary." *Post and Courier*. Last modified May 13, 2019. https://www.postandcourier.com/politics/the-safe-choice-biden -widens-sc-lead-in-democratic-presidential/article_f727895c-731f-11e9 -888a-af4280777b2a.html.

19. "Endorsements in the 2020 Democratic Party Presidential Primaries." Wikipedia. Last modified March 25, 2019. https://en.wikipedia.org/wiki /Endorsements_in_the_2020_Democratic_Party_presidential_primaries #Joe_Biden.

20. Kurtz, Judy. "Rob Reiner Backs Biden's 2020 Bid." *The Hill*. Last modified April 25, 2019. https://thehill.com/blogs/in-the-know/in-the-know/440728 -rob-reiner-backs-bidens-2020-bid.

21. Samuels, Brett. "Author George RR Martin Backs Biden's Candidacy." *The Hill.* Last modified May 6, 2019. https://thehill.com/blogs/in-the-know/in-the-know/442280-george-rr-martin-backs-bidens-candidacy.

22. "Election 2020 - General Election: Trump vs. Biden." *RealClearPolitics.* Accessed June 3, 2019. https://www.realclearpolitics.com/epolls/2020/president/us/general_election_trump_vs_biden-6247.html.

23. University, Quinnipiac. "QU Poll Release Detail." *QU Poll.* Accessed June 3, 2019. https://poll.qu.edu/pennsylvania/release-detail?ReleaseID=2620.

24. Allen, Jonathan. "Why the 2020 Democratic Primary Could Turn into 'Lord of the Flies.'" *NBC News.* Last modified January 24, 2019. https://www.nbcnews.com/politics/2020-election/why-2020-democratic-primary-could-turn-lord-flies-n961236.

25. Drucker, David M. "'It's a Gold Mine of Content?: Inside the GOP Operation to Take Down Biden." *The Hive.* Last modified May 23, 2019. https://www.vanityfair.com/news/2019/05/inside-the-gop-operation-to-take-down-joe-biden.

26. Easley, Jonathan. "Poll: 60 Percent Say Trump Should Not Be Reelected." *The Hill.* Last modified May 22, 2019. https://thehill.com/homenews/administration/444972-poll-60-percent-say-trump-should-not-be-reelected.